Visual Reference

Microsoft®

Access 97

At a Glance

Microsoft Press

Published by **Microsoft Press**
A Division of Microsoft Corporation
One Microsoft Way
Redmond, Washington 98052-6399

Library of Congress Cataloging-in-Publication Data
Microsoft Access 97 at a glance / Perspection, Inc.
     p.   cm.
  Includes index.
  ISBN 1-57231-369-2
  1. Database management.   2. Microsoft Access.
  I. Perspection, Inc.
  QA76.9.D3M5565 1996
  005.75'65--dc20
                               96-36628
                                     CIP

Printed and bound in the United States of America.

3 4 5 6 7 8 9 QEQE 1 0 9 8

Distributed to the book trade in Canada by Macmillan of Canada, a division of Canada Publishing Corporation.

A CIP catalogue record for this book is available from the British Library.

Microsoft Press books are available through booksellers and distributors worldwide. For further information about international editions, contact your local Microsoft Corporation office. Or contact Microsoft Press International directly at fax (206) 936-7329.

Microsoft, Microsoft Press, MS-DOS, Microsoft Access, FoxPro, and Windows are registered trademarks of Microsoft Corporation. Other product and company names mentioned herein may be the trademarks of their respective owners.

Companies, names, and/or data used in screens and sample output are fictitious unless otherwise noted.

For Perspection, Inc.
Managing Editor: **Steven M. Johnson**
Writer: **Marie Swanson**
Production Editor: **David W. Beskeen**
Copy Editor: **Jane Pedicini**
Technical Editors: **Ann-Marie Buconjic**
                     Christine Spillett

For Microsoft Press
Acquisitions Editors: **Lucinda Rowley, Kim Fryer**
Project Editor: **Lucinda Rowley**

Contents

"How can I get started quickly in Access?"

see page 8

Get help with the
Office Assistant
see page 16

Search for text
in records
see page 34

*"I want to speed
up searches in
my database."*

see page 68

8 Maintaining Database Information   **89**

9 Creating Reports   **109**

*"How can I set
field properties
correctly?"*

see page 88

A B C

Enter Data
More Accurately
see page 96

"I want to create a data entry form quickly and easily."

see page 132

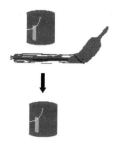

Add lines, borders, and colors to forms and reports see pages 152-155

Insert a Graph chart
see page 172

13 Accessing the Internet 177

Insert hyperlinks
see pages 214-215

14 Maximizing Database Performance 195

"How can I record and run a macro?"

see pages 226-229

Acknowledgments

The task of creating any book requires the talents of many hard-working people pulling together to meet impossible deadlines and untold stresses. We'd like to thank the outstanding team responsible for making this book possible: the writer, Marie Swanson, the editor, Kathy Finnegan, the copy editor, Jane Pedicini, the technical editors, Ann Marie Buconjic and Christine Spillett, the production team, Steven Payne, Patrica Young, and Gary Bedard, and the indexer, Michael Brackney.

At Microsoft Press, we'd like to thank Lucinda Rowley for the opportunity to undertake this project and Kim Eggleston for production expertise with the At a Glance series.

Perspection

Perspection

Perspection, Inc. is a technology training company committed to providing information to help people communicate, make decisions, and solve problems. Perspection writes and produces software training books, and develops interactive multimedia applications for Windows-based and Macintosh personal computers.

Microsoft Access 97 At a Glance incorporates Perspection's training expertise to ensure that you'll receive the maximum return on your time. With this staightforward, easy-to-read reference tool you'll get the information you need when you need it. You'll focus on the skills that increase productivity while working at your own pace and convenience.

We invite you to visit the Perspection World Wide Web site. You can visit us at:

http://www.perspection.com

You'll find a description for all of our books, additional content for our books, information about Perspection, and much more.

About
At a Glance

Microsoft *Access 97 At a Glance* is for anyone who wants to get the most from their computer and their software with the least amount of time and effort. You'll find this book to be a straightforward, easy-to-read reference tool. With the premise that your computer should work for you, not you for it, this book's purpose is to help you get your work done quickly and efficiently so that you can get away from the computer and live your life.

No Computerese!

Let's face it—when there's a task you don't know how to do but you need to get it done in a hurry, or when you're stuck in the middle of a task and can't figure out what to do next, there's nothing more frustrating than having to read page after page of technical background material. You want the information you need—nothing more, nothing less—and you want it now! And it should be easy to find and understand.

That's what this book is all about. It's written in plain English—no technical jargon and no computerese. There's no single task in the book that takes more than two pages. Just look up the task in the index or the table of contents, turn to the page, and there's the information, laid out step by step and accompanied by a graphic that adds visual clarity. You don't get bogged down by the whys and wherefores; just follow the steps, look at the illustrations, and get your work done with a minimum of hassle.

Occasionally you might want to turn to another page if the procedure you're working on has a "See Also" in the left column. That's because there's a lot of overlap among tasks, and we didn't want to keep repeating ourselves. We've also scattered some useful tips here and there, and thrown in a "Try This" once in a while, but by and large we've tried to remain true to the heart and soul of the book, which is that information you need should be available to you at a glance.

Useful Tasks...

Whether you use Access 97 for work, play, or some of each, we've tried to pack this book with procedures for everything we could think of that you might want to do, from the simplest tasks to some of the more esoteric ones.

...And the Easiest Way To Do Them

Another thing we've tried to do in *Access 97 At a Glance* is to find and document the easiest way to accomplish a task. Access often provides many ways to accomplish a single end result, which can be daunting or delightful, depending on the way you like to work. If you tend to stick with one favorite and familiar approach, we think the methods described in this book are the way to go. If you like trying out alternative techniques, go ahead! The intuitiveness of Access invites exploration, and you're likely to discover ways of doing things that you think are easier or that you like better. If you do, that's great! It's exactly what the creators of

Access 97 had in mind when they provided so many alternatives.

A Quick Overview

This book isn't meant to be read in any particular order. It's designed so that you can jump in, get the information you need, and then close the book and keep it near your computer until the next time you need it. But that doesn't mean we scattered the information about with wild abandon. If you were to read the book from front to back, you'd find a logical progression from the simple tasks to the more complex ones. Here's a quick overview.

First, we assume that Access 97 is already installed on your machine. If it's not, the Setup Wizard makes installation so simple that you won't need our help anyway. So, unlike most computer books, this one doesn't start out with installation instructions and a list of system requirements. You've already got that under control.

Sections 2 and 3 of the book cover the basics: starting Microsoft Access 97; working with menus, toolbars, and dialog boxes; opening, viewing, and modifying tables; and moving to records in tables.

Sections 4 through 6 describe tasks that are useful for locating and viewing records: searching for text in records; viewing specific records using filters; and creating queries to add records, create new tables, delete records, and update records.

Section 7 and 8 describe tasks that are essential to creating and maintaining databases: planning and creating databases; creating tables and setting up properties; entering records; and importing and exporting data.

Sections 9 through 12 describe tasks that are important for creating forms and reports: creating forms and reports from scratch and using wizards; modifying forms and reports in Design view; formatting forms and reports using lines, borders, colors, and special effects; and adding graphics, clip art, maps, and charts to forms and reports.

Section 13 describes tasks that are useful for accessing the Internet from Microsoft Access: inserting hyperlinks in forms, reports, and fields; navigating hyperlinks using the Web toolbar; searching for information and getting media clips on the Web; and publishing Internet ready databases.

Section 14 describes tasks that are helpful for maximizing performance and managing databases: analyzing databases for maximum performance; setting up accounts and permissions; securing databases; and repairing and replicating databases.

Section 15 covers information that isn't vital to using Access, but will help you work more efficiently, such as creating shortcuts on the desktop, setting Access options, recording and running macros, and customizing toolbars and toolbar buttons.

A Final Word (or Two)

We had three goals in writing this book, and here they are:

- ◆ Whatever you want to do, we want the book to help you get it done.

- ◆ We want the book to help you discover how to do things you *didn't* know you wanted to do.

- ◆ And, finally, if we've achieved the first two goals, we'll be well on the way to the third, which is for our book to help you enjoy doing your work with Access 97. We think that would be the best gift we could give you as a "thank you" for buying our book.

We hope you'll have as much fun using *Access 97 At a Glance* as we've had writing it. The best way to learn is by doing, and that's what we hope you'll get from this book.

Jump right in!

2

Microsoft Access 97 Database Basics

Microsoft Access 97 is a database program that allows you to:

◆ Store an almost limitless amount of information

◆ Organize information in a way that makes sense for how you work

◆ Retrieve information based on selection criteria you specify

◆ Create forms that make it easier to enter information

◆ Generate meaningful and insightful reports that can combine data, text, graphics, and even sound

What Is a Database?

Database is a rather technical word for a collection of information that is organized as a list. This definition might be oversimplified, but essentially whenever you use or make a list of information—names, addresses, products, customers, or invoices—you are using a database. A database that you store on your computer, however, is much more flexible and powerful than a simple list you keep on paper, in your cardfile, or in your address book.

Understanding Access Databases

In Access, a database consists of tables, their relationship to one another (if any), reports, queries, filters, forms, and macros.

Parts of a database

Tables are where you store information related to a specific part of your business or work. For example, the Northwind database contains a table of customer information. Another table stores purchasing information, and still another table contains product information. Tables are organized into rows and columns. Each row represents a set of information called a *record*. In the Customers table in the Northwind database, for example, each row represents a customer record, which is the information related to a specific customer. Columns represent a specific piece of information, called a *field*. For example, in the Customers table, the customer's company name is stored in the Company Name field.

In addition you can relate the tables to each other based on a field the tables have in common. By relating two tables to each other, you can work with data from both tables as if they were one larger table.

A table with rows and columns

To locate information in a table (or in multiple tables) you create a query. A *query* is simply a question you ask of a database to help you locate specific information. For example, if you want to know which customers placed orders in the last six months, you can create a query in which you ask Access to examine the contents of the Order Date field in the Orders table and to find all the records in which the purchase date is less than six months ago.

Queries in a database

After Access has retrieved the records that match the specifications in your query, you can sort or filter the information with still more specific criteria, so that you can focus on exactly the information you need—no more or less.

To make it easier to enter information into your tables, you can create customized *forms* that direct you to enter the correct information, check it for errors, and then store the information in the proper table. A form usually displays all the fields for one record at a time, making it easier for you to focus on a particular record.

A form in Access

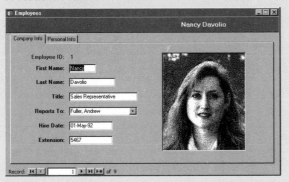

After you have retrieved and organized only the specific information you want, you can display and print this information as a *report*. In Access you can create a simple report that displays each record's information, or you can customize a report to include calculations, charts, graphics, and other features to go beyond the numbers and really emphasize the information in the report.

A report in Access

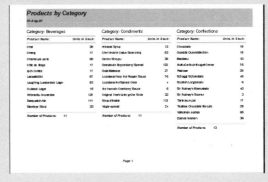

To automate a series of Access commands, you can create a *macro*. With macros, you can perform a series of commands with a click of a button.

In addition, you can automate many Access database procedures and combine them with Microsoft Visual Basic programs to create modules. *Modules* allow you to expand upon and integrate Access commands and macros with Microsoft Visual Basic, as well as other Microsoft Office 97 programs.

Starting Microsoft Access 97

Before you can use Access, you need to start Windows 95. Then you can start Access using the Start button on the taskbar. If you have installed Access as part of the Microsoft Office 97 suite of programs, you can start Access from the Office menu command or Shortcut Bar. After you start the program, you see the Microsoft Access dialog box in the program window. This dialog box opens whenever you start Access.

SEE ALSO

See "Opening a Database" on page 5 for more information about using the Microsoft Access dialog box.

Start Access from the Start Menu

1. Click the Start button on the taskbar to display the Start menu.

2. Point to Programs to display the Programs menu.

3. Click Microsoft Access.

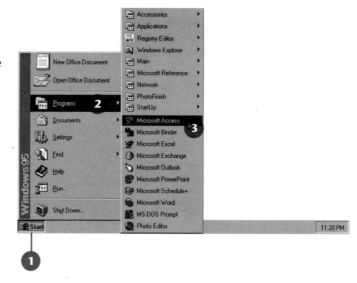

Start Access by Opening a New Database

1. Click the Start button on the taskbar, and then click New Office Document.

2. Click the General tab.

3. Click the Blank Database icon.

4. Click OK. Before you can begin working on your new database, you'll need to give it a name.

5. Type a database name in the File name list box, and then click Create.

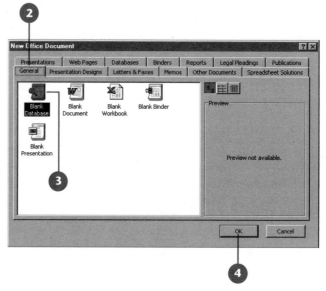

Opening a Database

To work in Access, you first need to open an existing database file or create a new database. To better illustrate the basic skills of using a database, you can begin learning to use Access by opening the sample Northwind database provided with Access. If you want to work in your own database, you can still follow these instructions.

TIP

Open a recently used database quickly and easily. *If the database you want to open is one of the last four databases you worked on, you can open the database by selecting it from the bottom of the File menu in the Microsoft Access program window. Just click the File menu, and then click the name of the database you want to open.*

Open a Database from the Access Dialog Box

1 In the Microsoft Access dialog box, click the Open An Existing Database option button.

2 Double-click the name of the database you want to open. If the database is not listed, double-click More Files to display the Open dialog box, and then select the database you want to open.

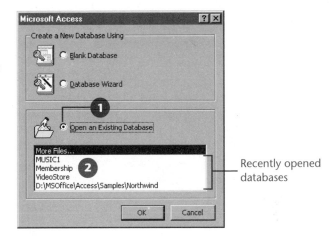

Recently opened databases

Open a Database from the Program Window

1 Click the Open Database button on the Database toolbar.

2 Select the drive and folder containing the database you want to open.

3 Double-click the database you want to open.

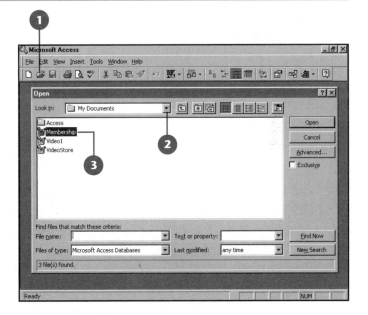

Viewing the Access Window

The *Title bar* displays the name of the open program.

The *Menu bar* contains menu items that represent groups of related commands.

The *Toolbar* contains buttons that you click to carry out commands.

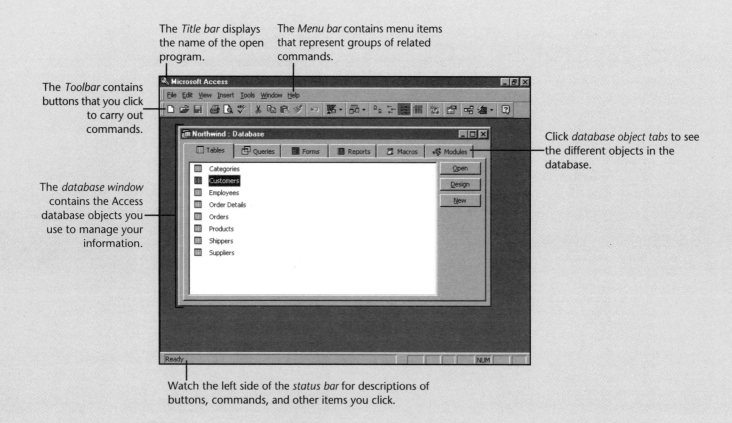

The *database window* contains the Access database objects you use to manage your information.

Click *database object tabs* to see the different objects in the database.

Watch the left side of the *status bar* for descriptions of buttons, commands, and other items you click.

Working with Menus and Toolbars

You can perform most Access functions by choosing menu options and clicking toolbar buttons. A toolbar contains buttons you can click to carry out commands you use most frequently. When you place the mouse pointer over a toolbar button, the name of the button appears in a small box called a *ScreenTip*.

Select a Menu Command

1 Click a menu name on the menu bar.

2 Click a command to perform the command, or point to a command followed by an arrow to see a submenu of related options, and then click the command you want.

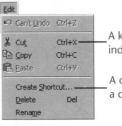

A dimmed command is not available at the moment.

A keyboard command next to a command indicates a keyboard shortcut.

A command followed by an ellipsis (...) displays a dialog box containing more options.

Display a ScreenTip and Select a Toolbar Command

1 Position the mouse pointer over a toolbar button and wait a moment.

The name of the button appears.

2 Click a toolbar button to perform the command.

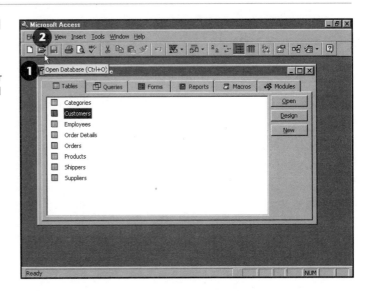

Working with Dialog Boxes

Commands that are followed by an ellipsis (...) display a dialog box. A *dialog box* is a special window in which you can specify additional options for carrying out a command. You make your choices by typing in text boxes, clicking option buttons and check boxes, or clicking options from a drop-down list.

TIP

Test your dialog box changes. *If a dialog box contains an Apply button, it means you can click this button to apply the changes without closing the dialog box. You can see the results of your changes and make additional changes as needed with the dialog box open.*

Select Dialog Box Options

A dialog box can consist of one or more of the following features:

- ◆ Tabs
- ◆ Option buttons
- ◆ Drop-down lists
- ◆ Text boxes
- ◆ Check boxes

After you enter information or make selections in a dialog box, click OK to carry out your selections. Or click Cancel to close the dialog box and cancel your selections.

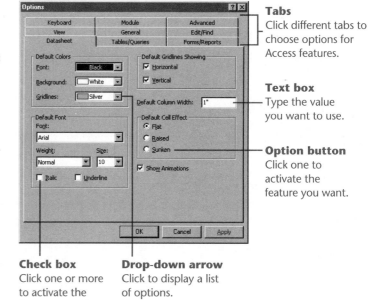

Tabs
Click different tabs to choose options for Access features.

Text box
Type the value you want to use.

Option button
Click one to activate the feature you want.

Check box
Click one or more to activate the features you want.

Drop-down arrow
Click to display a list of options.

Getting Help Using the Help Pointer

A quick way to learn about Access features is to use the What's This? command on the Help menu. When you choose this command, the pointer changes to the *Help pointer*. With the Help pointer you can click different features and items to get information about that item. Some dialog boxes contain a Help button. Clicking the Help button in a dialog box works the same way as clicking the What's This? command on the Help menu.

Help button

Get Help with the Help Pointer

1. Click the Help menu, and then click What's This?

2. Click the Help pointer on the item about which you want more information.

3. Click anywhere on the screen to close the Help information box.

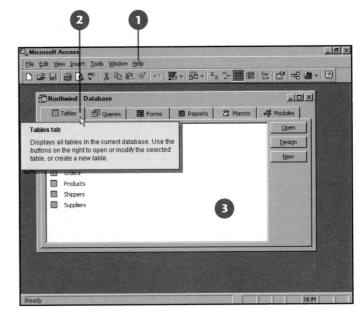

Get Help in a Dialog Box

1. Open a dialog box.

2. Click the Help button.

3. Click the Help pointer on the item in the dialog box about which you want more information.

4. Click anywhere on the screen to close the Help information box.

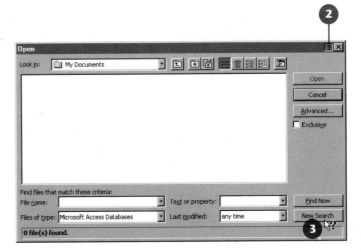

Getting Help Using the Help Dialog Box

The Access Help system provides much of the information you would expect to find in a manual or book, and in a convenient form—on your computer screen. You can quickly get the information you need with the Contents And Index command on the Help menu. You can look up general Help topics using the Contents tab or more specific topics using the Index tab. The Find tab allows you to look for specific words and phrases in Help topics.

Get Help Using the Help Topics List

1 Click the Help menu, and then click Contents And Index to display the Help Topics dialog box.

2 On the Contents tab, double-click the topic you want to see.
You can open as many topics as you want.

3 Click a topic, and then click Display.

4 Click any labels in the window to get more information.

5 Click Help Topics to return to the Contents tab.

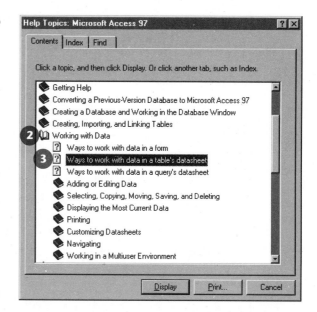

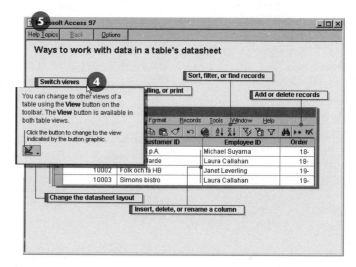

Locate specific text in a Help window. *Click the Help menu, and then click Contents And Index. Click the Find tab and type the text you want to locate. Access will display a list of topics that contain the text you typed. Select a topic and click Display.*

Change the way Help works. *Click the Options button (or click the right mouse button and choose Options) in a Help topic window to see a list of options available when you are using Help. These options allow you to enter annotated comments for a Help topic, copy and print Help information, change the font size of text in the Help window, and change the location and colors of the Help window.*

Search for Help Information

1. Click the Help menu, and then click Contents And Index to display the Help Topics dialog box.

2. Click the Index tab.

3. In the text box, type the feature about which you want more information.

4. In the list of index entries, click the topic you want.

5. Click Display to see a list of topics that are related to your selection.

6. In the Topics Found dialog box, click the topic you want to see.

7. Click Display and read the topic.

8. Click Help Topics to return to the Index tab.

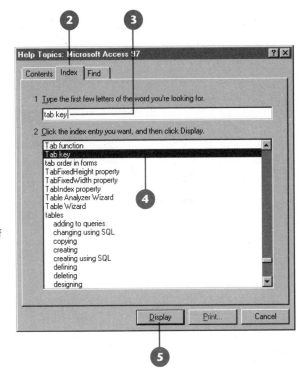

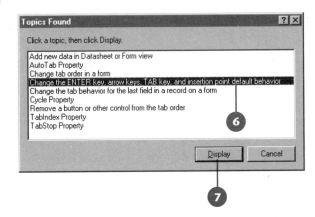

Getting Help Using the Office Assistant

If you have installed Access as part of Office 97, you can display the Office Assistant as you work. With the *Office Assistant* displayed, the answers to your questions about using Access are never far away. You can also use the Office Assistant to automatically display helpful tips while you are working in Access. You can change the way the Office Assistant works to suit your needs and preferences.

Office Assistant button

Get Help with the Office Assistant

1 Click the Office Assistant button on the toolbar (if the Office Assistant is not already displayed). If the Office Assistant is displayed, click the Office Assistant to activate it.

2 Type your question in the space provided.

3 Click Search.

Access searches for topics that are related to the question you asked.

4 Double-click a topic.

Access displays a Help window.

5 Click an underlined word or phrase to display a definition.

6 Click the Close button on the Help window title bar to close the window.

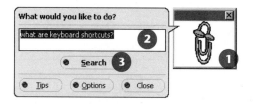

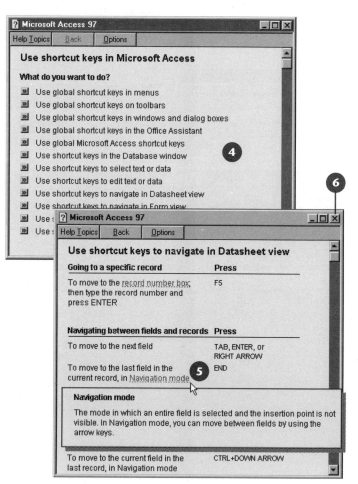

Display Tips with the Office Assistant

1 Click the Office Assistant button on the toolbar or click the Office Assistant to activate it.

2 Click Tips to display the tip window.

3 Click Back and Next to display the previous and next tips.

4 Click Close to close the tip window.

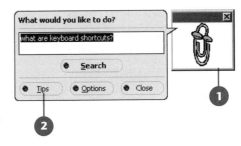

What would you like to do?

what are keyboard shortcuts?

● Search

● Tips ● Options ● Close

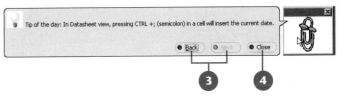

Tip of the day: In Datasheet view, pressing CTRL +; (semicolon) in a cell will insert the current date.

● Back ● Next ● Close

2

Change the Office Assistant character. *You can change the appearance of the Office Assistant. Click the Office Assistant, and then click the Options button. Click the Gallery tab, and then use the Back and Next buttons to scroll through the list of available characters to choose the one you want.*

Change Office Assistant Options

1 Click the Office Assistant button on the toolbar or click the Office Assistant to activate it.

2 Click Options to display the Office Assistant dialog box.

3 On the Options tab, click the check boxes for the Office Assistant features you want to activate or deactivate.

4 Click the Gallery tab if you want to select a different character as the Office Assistant.

5 Click OK to close the dialog box.

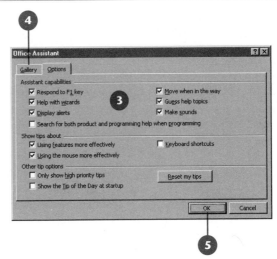

Office Assistant

Gallery Options

Assistant capabilities
☑ Respond to F1 key   ☑ Move when in the way
☑ Help with wizards   ☑ Guess help topics
☑ Display alerts   ☑ Make sounds
☐ Search for both product and programming help when programming

Show tips about
☑ Using features more effectively   ☐ Keyboard shortcuts
☑ Using the mouse more effectively

Other tip options
☐ Only show high priority tips   Reset my tips
☐ Show the Tip of the Day at startup

OK   Cancel

Closing a Database and Exiting Access

After you finish working in a database, you can close it. You can then choose to open another database or exit Access. If you made any changes to the structure of the database—for example, if you changed the size of any rows or columns in a table—Access prompts you to save your changes. Any changes you make to the data in a table are saved automatically as you make them. When you close a database or when you exit Access, any objects that are still open, such as tables or queries, will also be closed.

> **TIP**
>
> **Close the database, not Access.** *Be careful not to click the Close button on the title bar of the program window. Clicking this button will close the Access program.*

Close a Database

1 Click the Close button on the Database window.

2 Click No to ignore any changes you might have made to the database structure, or click Yes to save any changes you made.

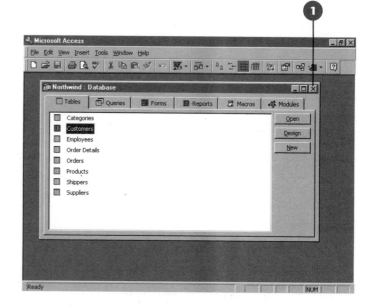

Exit Access

1 Click the File menu, and then click Exit or click the Close button on the title bar of the Access window.

2 Click No to ignore any changes you might have made to the database structure, or click Yes to save any changes you made.

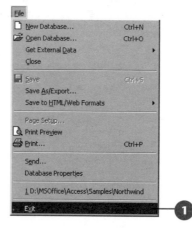

Working with Database Tables

The table is the primary element for your work in a database. A *table* contains the information you want to keep track of and retrieve. The information in a table is organized in fields (displayed as columns) and records (displayed as rows). A *field* is a specific item of data, such as a customer number, state, phone number, or company name. A *record* is a set of related fields about a specific individual, customer, company, or product. On the Tables tab in the Database window, you can see a list of all the tables in the database. By learning several ways to customize what you see when you view a table, you can work more effectively with the contents of a table.

For example, you can adjust the width and height of columns and rows to make the table easier to read. You can adjust the overall size of the Table window to see as much of the table as you need. Because you can open multiple tables at the same time, you can arrange the Table windows so you can see all the windows at once, or display each table one at a time. You can scroll to specific records you want to see and you can use other features to actually select specific records.

Opening and Closing Tables

To see the contents of a table, you must open it from the Database window. When you open a table it appears in the Table window in Datasheet view. *Datasheet view* shows the table's contents arranged in rows and columns. Each row represents a record. Each column represents a field. If you organize information into multiple tables, each containing records related to a specific part of the database, Access can process information more efficiently. You can open multiple tables in the program window at one time. Each table you open appears in a different Table window.

Open a Table

1. With the Database window open, click the Tables tab.

2. Double-click the name of the table you want to open.

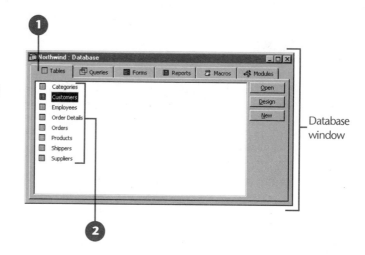

Database window

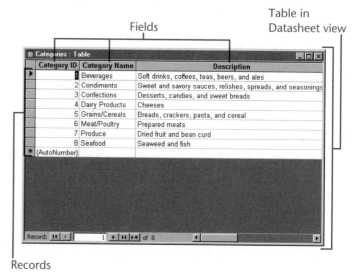

Fields

Table in Datasheet view

Records

Hide a Table window without closing it. *Click the Minimize button in the upper right corner of the Table window you want to hide. Clicking this button reduces the window to a minimized window at the bottom of the program window. To restore the Table window to its original size, click the Restore button.*

Close a Table

1 Click the Close button in the upper right corner of the Table window you want to close.

2 Click Yes to save any changes you made, or click No to ignore any changes you might have made to the table structure.

Clicking this button closes the Access program.

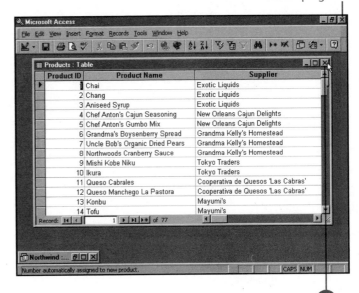

Viewing Multiple Tables

When you open multiple tables at once, you can arrange the Table windows so that you can see all open tables at the same time. For example, you can use the Tile Horizontally command on the Window menu to display the Table windows one above the other or you can use the Tile Vertically command to display the windows side by side. Each Table window contains scroll bars so that you can move around in each table. When you want several tables open but prefer to see only one at a time, you can use the Cascade command. This command staggers the arrangement of Table windows, so that the active Table window remains on top of a stack of windows.

TIP

Switch between open tables. *Click any visible part of a Table window. If one table obscures the other, you also can choose a table from the Window menu.*

View Multiple Tables

1 Click the Window menu, and then click:

- ◆ Tile Vertically to display Table windows side by side.

- ◆ Tile Horizontally to display Table windows one above the other.

- ◆ Cascade to display Table windows stacked and offset so, that you can see the title bars of the other windows.

2 Click any part of a window to make it active.

Active title bar

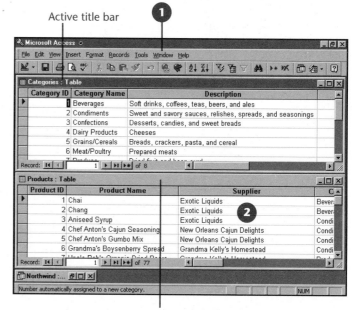

Inactive title bar

Sizing Tables

You can adjust the size of each window to fit your needs. For example, you can make a Table window larger, smaller, wider, narrower, or taller by dragging a window border in the direction you want to go. You can also minimize a window to, in effect, hide the window at the bottom of the screen, maximize a window to make it fill the screen, or restore a window to its original size. The buttons for minimizing, maximizing, and restoring windows are available in both the Access program window and in individual object windows.

TIP

Quickly switch between restored and maximized windows. *Double-click the title bar in a window to quickly switch between maximized and restored window sizes.*

Resize a Table Window

◆ Minimize a window:

Click the Minimize button to reduce the window to display only its name at the bottom of the program window.

◆ Restore a window:

Click the Restore button to restore the window to its original size.

◆ Maximize a window:

Click the Maximize button to display the window so that it fills the entire screen.

◆ Resize a window:

Position the pointer over a border. When you see the two-sided arrow, drag in the direction you want.

  ◆ Drag a side border to change the width of the window.

  ◆ Drag a top or bottom border to change the height of the window.

  ◆ Drag a corner border to change the size of the entire window.

◆ Move a window:

Drag the window's title bar to move the window to a new location.

Title bar   Minimize button   Restore button

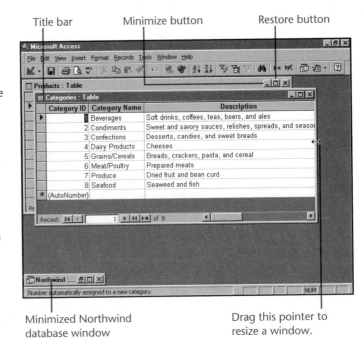

Minimized Northwind database window

Drag this pointer to resize a window.

Scrolling Through a Table

Depending on the size and resolution of your computer screen, you can see only a few records in your table at a time. Even if you increase the size of the Table window in Datasheet view, you won't be able to see all the records or fields in a very large table. One way to see the parts of a table that are not immediately in view is to scroll in the window using the scroll bars at the bottom and right edge of the window.

TIP

When you can scroll through a table. *Scroll bars appear in the Table window only if the table contains more information than is currently visible in the window.*

Scroll Through a Table

◆ Drag the vertical scroll box to display records located in another part of the table.

◆ Use the vertical scroll bar to scroll through records in a window.

◆ Drag the horizontal scroll box to display fields located in another part of the table.

◆ Use the horizontal scroll bar to scroll sideways through a window.

◆ Click a scroll arrow to scroll one record or field at a time.

Vertical scroll bar — Scroll box

Scroll arrow — Horizontal scroll bar

USING THE SCROLL BAR	
To:	**Do this:**
Scroll down one record the window	Click the arrow at the bottom of the in vertical scroll bar.
Scroll down one windowful of records	Click in the area below the scroll box in the vertical scroll bar.
Scroll one column to the right in the window	Click the arrow at the right of the horizontal scroll bar.
Scroll several columns to the right in the window	Click in the area to the right of the scroll box in the horizontal scroll bar.
Scroll to the first column in the table	Drag the scroll box in the horizontal scroll bar all the way to the left.
Scroll to the first record in the table	Drag the scroll box in the vertical scroll bar all the way to the top.
Scroll to the last column in the table	Drag the scroll box in the horizontal scroll bar all the way to the right.
Scroll to the last record in the table	Drag the scroll box in the vertical scroll bar all the way to the bottom.

Rearranging Columns

The order in which columns appear in the Table window in Datasheet view is initially determined by the order established when you first designed the table. If you want to temporarily rearrange the order of the columns in a table, you can do so without changing the table design. You can arrange columns in the order you want by selecting and then dragging columns to a new location.

SEE ALSO

See "Changing the Size of Rows and Columns" on page 28 for more information about working with rows and columns.

Move a Column

1 Select a column by clicking its column heading.

2 Position the mouse pointer over the selected column, and then press and hold the mouse button until the pointer changes shape.

3 Drag the column heading with the pointer to the right of where you want the column to appear.

4 Release the mouse button to place the column in its new position.

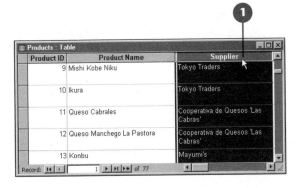

The highlighted vertical bar indicates the new position of the column.

Freezing and Unfreezing Columns

Each time you scroll a table to the right by one column, a column scrolls out of view on the left. With the *freeze column* feature, you can specify the columns that will not scroll out of view even when you continue to scroll to the right in a table. This feature is useful if you always want to display specific columns that contain important information. For example, you might want to freeze a Customer ID column so that you can verify that you are working in the correct record for a particular customer as you view or edit additional columns. Of course, if you decide you no longer need to freeze a column, you can always unfreeze it.

Freeze a Column

1. Select the column or columns you want to freeze by clicking the column heading or dragging the pointer to select multiple column headings.

2. Click the Format menu, and then click Freeze Columns.

The column remains in the window even as you scroll to the right.

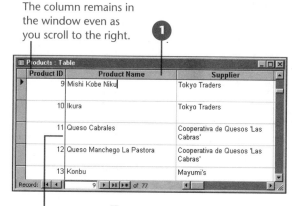

The dark column border indicates a frozen column.

Unfreeze a Column

1. Click the Format menu, and then click Unfreeze All Columns.

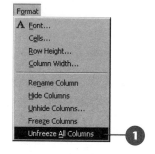

Hiding and Displaying Columns

To minimize the amount of scrolling you do as you work in a table, you might decide that you want to focus on certain columns and not be distracted by other columns you don't need at the moment. Using the hide and unhide columns features, you can selectively hide and display columns as you want.

SEE ALSO

See "Freezing and UnFreezing Columns" on page 26 for more information about modifying column display.

Hide a Column

1 Select the column or columns you want to hide by clicking the column heading or dragging the pointer to select multiple column headings.

2 Click the Format menu, and then click Hide Columns.

Display a Hidden Column

1 Click the Format menu, and then click Unhide Columns.

2 Click the check box next to the name of the column (or columns) you want to display. The check box for each displayed column is checked; the check box for any hidden column is unchecked.

3 Click Close.

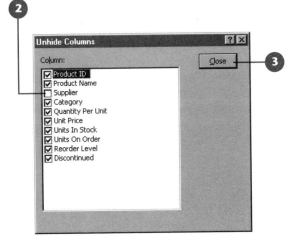

Changing the Size of Rows and Columns

If some of the text in a column is hidden because the column is too narrow, you can increase the width of the column to display more or all of the text in it. You can also change the height of the rows to provide more space for the text. Unlike changing the column width, which affects only the selected column or columns, changing the row height affects all the rows in the table. You can adjust the size of columns and rows by using commands or by dragging the mouse pointer.

TIP

You can change the default column width.
Click the Tools menu, and then click Options. On the Datasheet tab, specify the column width you want.

Change the Column Width

1 Position the insertion point anywhere in the column you want to change.

2 Click the Format menu, and then click Column Width.

3 Type the new width of the column.

4 Click OK.

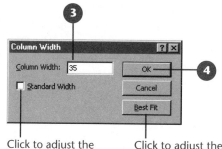

Click to adjust the width to the setting specified on the Datasheet tab in the Options dialog box.

Click to adjust the width to fit the field that contains the most text.

Drag to Change the Column Width

1 Position the pointer over the column border and drag the pointer to resize the column.

This column is being resized.

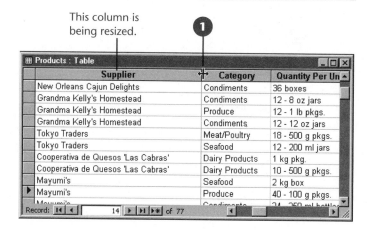

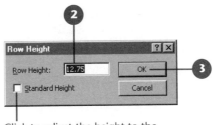

Change the Row Height

1 Click the Format menu, and then click Row Height.

2 Type the new row height for the rows in the table.

3 Click OK.

Click to adjust the height to the setting specified on the Datasheet tab in the Options dialog box.

Drag to Change the Row Height

1 Place the pointer over the row boundry and drag the pointer to adjust the height of all the rows in the table.

Moving to a Specific Record in a Table

When you scroll through a table in Datasheet view, you are simply viewing different parts of the table; the insertion point (cursor) stays in its original location in the first record. If you type any text, it would appear in the first record, regardless of which record is currently visible. To move the insertion point to a specific record, you must click the record (or a field in the record). If the record you want to select is not visible, you can use the navigation buttons to move to the next, previous, first, or last record. Or you can type the number of the record (if you know it) in the Specific Record box to move to that record. The Go To command also provides a fast way to move to a specific record.

Move to a Record Using the Mouse Button

◆ Current Record icon:

Indicates the current record.

◆ Specific Record box:

To move to a new record, select the current record number and then type the new record number.

◆ New Record button:

Click to create a new, blank row at the end of the table.

◆ Selection bar:

Click to the left of a record to select it.

◆ First Record button:

Click to move to the first record in the table.

◆ Previous Record button:

Click to move to the previous record in the table.

◆ Next Record button:

Click to move to the next record in the table.

◆ Last Record button:

Click to move to the last record in the table.

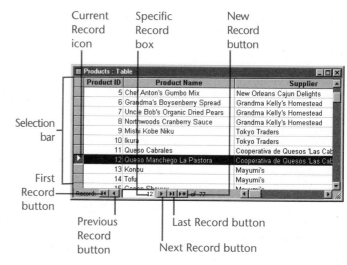

TRY THIS

Go to a specific record.

Experiment with the navigation buttons to move to different records in your table. Try using the Go To command to move to the second-to-last record in the table.

Move to a Specific Record Using the Go To Command

1 Click the Edit menu, and then click Go To.

2 Click the command that corresponds to the location of the record to which you want to move.

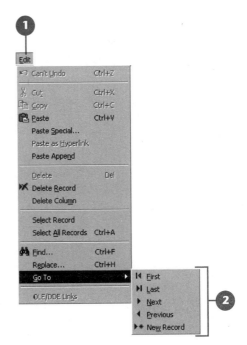

Locating and Viewing Specific Records

When you are working in a table that contains hundreds or even thousands of records, it can be a challenge to locate the exact information you want to see or use. Fortunately Microsoft Access 97 provides several ways for you to find and view the information you need:

◆ You can locate records based on text in the records. With the Find feature, you can move to the record you want by having Access search for the text you expect to find in the record. For example, if you want to locate records for customers in Canada, Access can search for the text "Canada" in all the records and move to the first one.

◆ You can arrange records in either ascending or descending order based on the contents of a specific field. For example, you can view records arranged alphabetically by customers' last names.

◆ To focus on certain records in a table, you can apply a filter to change which records are displayed. With a filter you describe characteristics or contents of the records you want to view, so that Access displays only those records that match the description.

Searching for Text in Records

To locate one or more records in which you expect to find specific text, you can use the Find feature. Using either the Find command on the Edit menu or the Find button on the Table Datasheet toolbar, you can enter the text you want to find and specify whether Access should search all the fields or just the current field, and where in the field the text should appear. You can also indicate whether the capitalization of the text Access finds should match the text you typed. When Access finds the first record that contains the specified text, it selects that record. You can then move to the next matching record or cancel the search.

Search for Text in the Current Field

1 Display the table in Datasheet view.

2 Click the insertion point anywhere in the field (column) where you expect to find the text for which you want to search.

3 Click the Find button on the Table Datasheet toolbar.

4 Type the text you want to find. You can enter the text in either uppercase or lowercase letters. If you want the text Access finds to match the capitalization of the text you enter, click the Match Case check box to select it; if not, clear the check box.

5 Click Find First to begin the search.

6 Click Find Next to move to subsequent records that contain the specified text.

7 Click Close to close the dialog box and return to the table in Datasheet view.

Clear this check box to ignore capitalization.

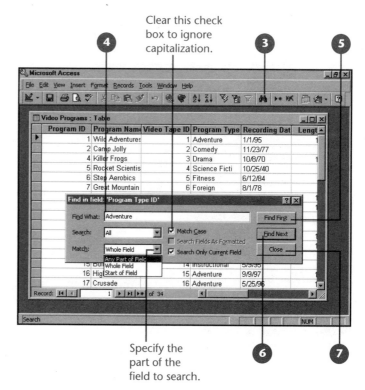

Specify the part of the field to search.

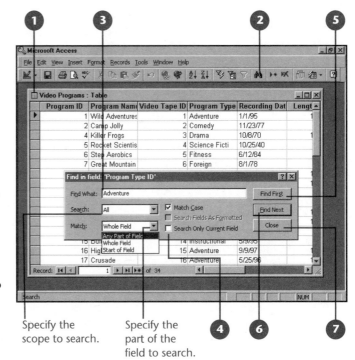

TIP

Search in either direction.
By default, Access searches the entire table. You can also search backwards through a table, ignoring any records following the current record. Or you can ignore the previous records and search only those records that appear after the current record. Click the Search drop-down arrow in the Find In Field dialog box to specify the direction of the search.

TIP

Specify the part of the field to search. *Access can search for text that matches text in any part of the field or at the beginning of the field, or Access can search for text that matches the entire field entry. Click the Match drop-down arrow in the Find In Field dialog box to specify the part of the field to search.*

Search for Text in All Fields

1 Display the table in Datasheet view.

2 Click the Find button on the Table Datasheet toolbar.

3 Type the text you want to find.

4 Clear the Search Only Current Field check box to search all the fields in the table.

5 Click Find First to begin the search.

6 Click Find Next to move to subsequent records that contain the specified text.

7 Click Close to close the dialog box and return to the table in Datasheet view.

Specify the scope to search.

Specify the part of the field to search.

4

Changing the Order of Records Displayed in a Table

You can change the order in which records appear in a table by *sorting* the records. You can select a field and then sort the records by the values in that field in either ascending or descending order. *Ascending* order means that records appear in alphabetical order (for text fields), from earliest to most recent (for date fields), or from smallest to largest (for numeric fields). *Descending* order means that records appear in reverse alphabetical order (for text fields), from most recent to earliest (for date fields), and from largest to smallest (for numeric fields). You can also change the order of records based on multiple fields.

Arrange Records in Ascending Order Based on One Field

1 Display the table in Datasheet view.

2 Position the insertion point anywhere in the field (column) that contains the values by which you want to sort the records.

3 Click the Sort Ascending button on the Table Datasheet toolbar.

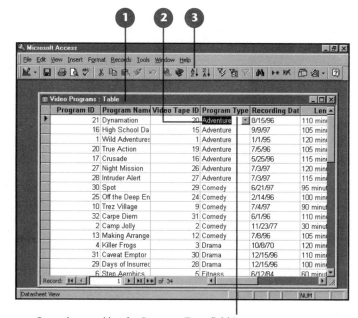

Records sorted by the Program Type field in ascending (alphabetical) order

TIP

Specify a sort order when designing a table. *Changing the order of records displayed in a table is not the same as specifying the sort order when you first design the table. Use the Sort feature when designing a table to display records in the order that you are likely to use most often, and then use the Sort Ascending and Sort Descending buttons to handle the exceptions when you display the table in Datasheet view.*

SEE ALSO

See "Viewing Specific Records Using a Filter" on page 40 for more information about the sort order of records in a table.

Arrange Records in Descending Order Based on One Field

1. Display the table in Datasheet view.

2. Position the insertion point anywhere in the field (column) that contains the values by which you want to sort the records.

3. Click the Sort Descending button on the Table Datasheet toolbar.

Records sorted by the Program Type field in descending (reverse alphabetical) order

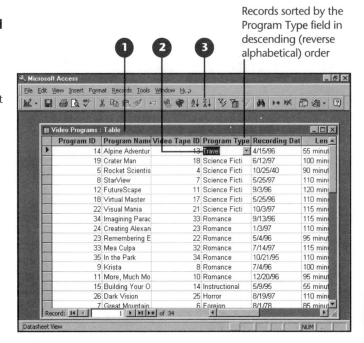

Arranging Records Based on Multiple Fields

When changing the order of records displayed in a table, you might need to sort the records by more than one field; this is referred to as a *secondary sort*. When you sort by more than one field, the fields must be next to each other in the table. After you select the fields, Access sorts them in order from left to right. For example, in a table containing information about video programs, you might need to view information about specific types of programs and the date on which each program was recorded. You could sort the records first by program type and then, in records with the same program type, sort the records by recording date.

Change the Order of Records Based on Multiple Fields

1 Display the table in Datasheet view.

2 Click the column heading of the first column you want to sort, and before you release the mouse button, drag the mouse to the right to highlight (select) the adjacent columns (fields).

3 Click the Sort Ascending button on the Table Datasheet toolbar to sort the records in ascending order, or click the Sort Descending button on the Table Datasheet toolbar to sort the records in descending order.

Within each type, records are sorted by the Recording Date field in descending order.

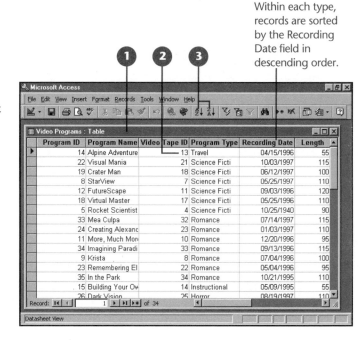

Finding and Replacing Text in a Table

When you are updating information in a table, you might need to make the same change to a number of records. You can use the Replace feature to locate each occurrence of specified text and change all occurrences to new text. You have the option to review and change each occurrence individually, or you can replace all occurrences at one time. As with the Find feature, you can specify the direction of the search, whether or not to match your capitalization, and whether or not to match the entire field or just part of it.

Find and Replace Text

1. Display the table in Datasheet view.

2. Click anywhere in the field (column) where you expect to find the text for which you want to search.

3. Click the Edit menu, and then click Replace.

4. In the Find What box, type the original text to replace.

5. In the Replace With box, type the new replacement text.

6. Click Find Next to locate the first occurrence.

7. Click Replace to replace the first occurrence with the replacement text; or click Replace All to replace all occurrences with the replacement text, or click Find Next to skip to the next occurrence.

8. Click Close when you have completed replacing text.

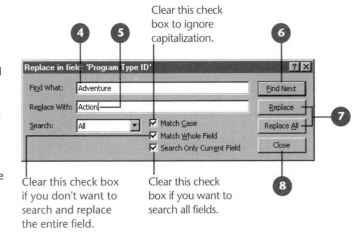

Clear this check box to ignore capitalization.

Clear this check box if you don't want to search and replace the entire field.

Clear this check box if you want to search all fields.

Viewing Specific Records Using a Filter

Instead of displaying all the records in a table, you can use a *filter* to display only those records that you want to see. You can display records based on a specific value in one field or on multiple values in multiple fields. You can filter by selecting the field value on which to base the filter in Datasheet view, or by using the Filter By Form feature to help you create more complex filters involving multiple field values. After you apply a filter, Access displays only those records that match your specifications. You can remove a filter to return the datasheet to its original display.

Filter By Selection button

Filter a Table by Selection

1. Display the table in Datasheet view.

2. Position the insertion point anywhere in the specific field value on which you want to base the filter.

3. Click the Filter By Selection button on the Table Datasheet toolbar. Notice that the bottom of the Table window tells you the number of records matching your filter criteria. Also the notation "FLTR" in the status bar indicates that a filter is currently in effect.

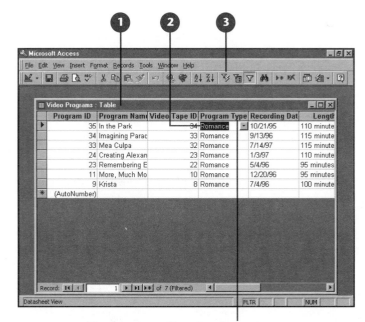

The records are filtered to show only the Romance program type.

Clear a Filter from a Table

1. Click the Apply Filter button on the Table Datasheet toolbar. Notice that the status bar removes the indication that the table is filtered.

Saving a Customized Filter

If you enter a series of criteria in a filter that you expect you might need again, or if you create a rather complex filter, consider saving the criteria as a query. In many ways, a query is simply a filter you have decided to save. However, queries also have other unique capabilities that extend beyond what you can accomplish in a filter. For now, however, you can create a simple query by saving a filter you have already created.

TIP

Run a filter that you saved as a query. *Click the Queries tab on the Database window, and then double-click the name of the filter that you saved as a query.*

SEE ALSO

See "Understanding the Different Types of Queries" on page 46 for more information about queries.

Save a Filter as a Query

1 Display the filtered table in Datasheet view.

2 Click the Records menu, point to Filter, and then click Advanced Filter/Sort. The details of the filter appear in Design view.

3 Click the File menu, and then click Save As Query.

4 In the Query Name box, type the name you want to assign to the query. If you enter the name of an existing query, Access will ask if you want to overwrite the existing query. Be sure to answer "No" if you want to retain the original query, so you can give the new query a different name.

5 Click OK to save the filter as a query. The query you have just saved appears on the Queries tab in the Database window.

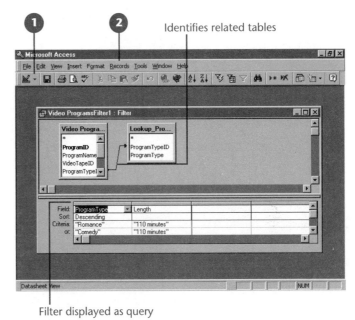

Identifies related tables

Filter displayed as query

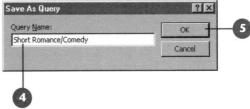

Creating More Complex Filters Using a Form

The *Filter By Form* feature allows you to create a more complex filter. The more criteria you provide on each tab of the form, the more restrictive your filter will be. Adding criteria on a particular tab in the form restricts the filter so that records must match *all* the criteria on the form for the records to be displayed; this is called an *AND filter*. To expand the filter to include more records, you can create an *OR filter* by specifying criteria on the subsequent Or tabs in the Filter By Form grid. A record needs to match only the criteria specified on the Look For tab or the criteria specified on anyone of the Or tab(s) to be displayed.

Apply Filter button

Create an AND Filter

1 Display the table in Datasheet view.

2 Click the Filter By Form button on the Table Datasheet toolbar.

3 If necessary, click the Clear Grid button on the Filter/ Sort toolbar to clear the previous filter.

4 Click in the empty text box below the field you want to filter.

5 Click the drop-down arrow for the current field, and then click the field value by which you want to filter the records. If you are specifying criteria for a text field type, you must type quotation marks around the field value in the Filter By Form grid in order for the filter to work correctly.

6 For each field by which you want to filter, click the drop-down arrow and select the entry for your filter. Each new field in which you make a selection adds additional criteria that a record must match to be included.

7 Click the Apply Filter button on the Filter/Sort toolbar.

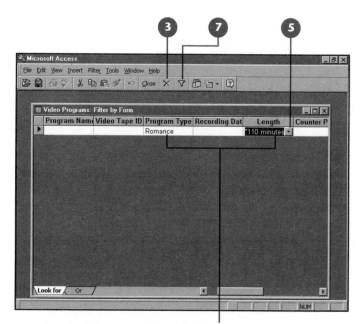

Criteria on the same tab for an AND filter.

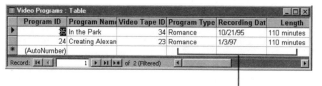

Only those records containing both criteria—a Program Type value of Romance and a Length value of 110 minutes—are displayed.

TIP

Save a filter you created. *If you create a complex or highly customized filter, you can save the filter as a query. Then you can open and run the query whenever you want to view the results of the filter and display only the information that you need at the moment.*

SEE ALSO

See "Saving a Customized Filter" on page 9 for more information about filters.

Create an OR Filter

1. Display the table in Datasheet view.

2. Click the Filter By Form button on the Table Datasheet toolbar.

3. If necessary, click the Clear Grid button on the Filter/ Sort toolbar to clear the previous filter.

4. Click the text box below the field you want to filter.

5. Click the drop-down arrow for the current field, and then click the field value by which you want to filter the records. If you are specifying criteria for a text field type, you must type quotation marks around the field value in the Filter By Form grid in order for the filter to work correctly.

6. For each field by which you want to filter, click the drop-down arrow and select the entry for your filter.

7. Click the Or tab at the bottom of the form to specify additional criteria for the filter.

8. Click the Apply Filter button on the Filter/Sort toolbar.

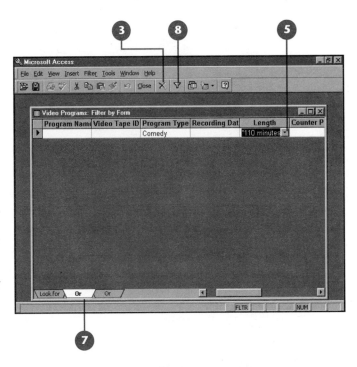

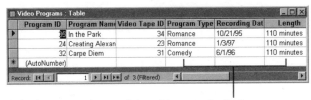

Only those records containing either set of criteria—a Program Type value of Romance and a Length value of 110 minutes *OR* a Program Type value of Comedy and a Length value of 110 minutes—are included in the display.

Retrieving Records from a Database

A *query* is a description of the records you want to retrieve from a Microsoft Access 97 database. As the name implies, a query helps answer specific questions about the information in your database—for example, "Which customers have placed orders in the last 6 months?" or "Who sent us greeting cards over the holidays in the last two years?" The description of the records you want to retrieve identifies the names of the fields and the values they should contain; this description is called the *selection criteria*. With a query you can:

◆ Specify which fields you want to include in the query results. This enables you to focus on only the information you need.

◆ Save a query definition—that is, the specifications of a query—so that you can use it again without having to re-create it.

◆ Save the records in the results of a query as a new table. This is a fast way to create new tables.

◆ Enter formulas and expressions using the information in the table.

◆ Retrieve information stored in multiple tables, even if the tables are not open.

Understanding the Different Types of Queries

There are several different types of queries you can use: select queries, crosstab queries, action queries, and parameter queries.

- A *select query* retrieves and displays records in the Table window in Datasheet view.

- A *crosstab query* displays summarized values (sums, counts, and averages) from one field in a table and groups them by one set of fields listed down the left side of the datasheet and another set of fields listed across the top of the datasheet.

- An *action query* performs operations on the records that match your criteria. There are four kinds of action queries: *delete queries* delete matching records from a table; *update queries* make changes to matching records in a table; *append queries* add new records to the end of a table (records not matching your criteria are added to the table); and *make-table* queries create new tables based on matching records.

- A *parameter query* allows you to prompt for a single piece of information to use as selection criteria in the query. For example, instead of creating separate queries to retrieve customer information for each state in which you do business, you could create a parameter query that prompts you to enter the name of a state, and then continues to retrieve those specific records from that state.

Creating Queries in Access

As with most objects you create in a database, you have several ways to create a query. You can create a query from scratch or use a wizard to guide you through the process of creating a query. With the Query Wizard, Microsoft Access helps you create a simple query to retrieve the records you want. All queries you create and save are listed on the Queries tab in the Database window. You can then double-click a query to run it and display the results. When you run a select query, the query results will show only the selected fields for each record in the table that matches your selection criteria. Of course, once you have completed a query, you can further customize it in Design view. As always, you can begin creating your query in Design view without using the wizard at all.

Query wizard dialog box

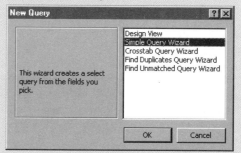

Creating a Query from Scratch

Although a wizard can be a big help when you are first learning to create a query, you do not need to use the wizard. If you prefer, you can create a query without the help of a wizard. Instead of answering questions in a series of dialog boxes, you can start working in Design view right away.

SEE ALSO

See "Displaying a Query in Design View" on page 56, "Changing the Fields in a Query" on page 50, "Comparing Values in Section Criteria" on page 58, and "Calculating Values in a Query" on page 60 for information on specifying fields, using conditions, and using the Expression Builder.

Create a Query from Scratch

1 In the Database window, click the Queries tab, and then click New.

2 In the New Query dialog box, click Design View, and then click OK.

3 Select the table or query containing the records you want to retrieve.

4 Click Add.

5 Repeat steps 3 and 4 for each table or query you want to use.

6 Click Close to display the query in Design view.

7 In the field list at the top part of the Design view window, double-click each field you want to include in the query.

8 In the Design grid, enter search criteria in the Criteria box.

9 Click the Sort drop-down arrow to specify a sort order for records when they appear in the query results.

10 Click the Save button on the Query Design toolbar, type a name for the query, and then click OK.

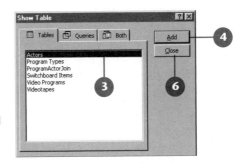

Click to run the query   Click to add new tables to the query

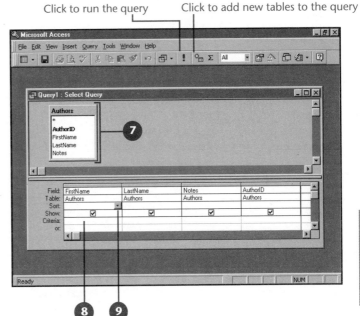

5

Creating a Query Using the Query Wizard

When you create a query, you can choose from several different kinds of queries. By choosing the Query Wizard, you can specify the records you want to retrieve and specify other kinds of queries you want to create. The Query Wizard guides you through each step. All you do is answer a series of questions about your query, and Access creates a query with your data.

Create a Query Using the Query Wizard

1 On the Queries tab in the Database window, click the New button, click the wizard that corresponds to the kind of query you want to create, and then clic OK.

2 Click the Tables/Queries drop-down arrow and select a table with fields to include in the query.

3 Click each available field that you want included in the query, and then click the Add button (>). To include all the available fields, click the Add All button (>>).

4 Click Next to continue.

5 If you have selected numeric or date fields in step 3, you can indicate whether you want to see detail or summary information. If you choose Summary, click Summary Options to specify the calculation for each field. Select averages, counts, and minimum and maximum values, and then click OK.

6 Click Next to continue.

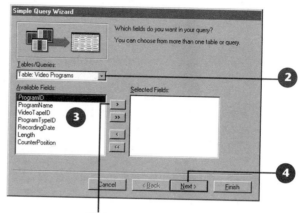

Click to add available fields to your query.

Click to specify the summary calculations.

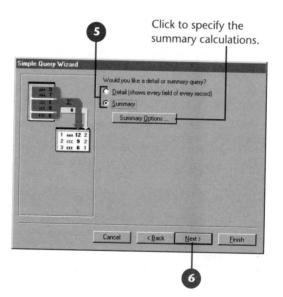

7 In the final wizard dialog box, type the name of the query.

8 Click an option to view the query results or display the query in Design view.

9 Click Finish.

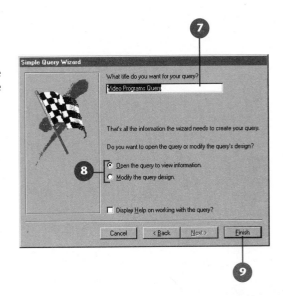

Records retrieved by a query

Changing the Fields in a Query

In Design view, you can add or remove fields in your query design to produce different results. You can also include fields from other tables in your database. In some cases you might want to hide a field from the query results while keeping it as part of the query design for selection criteria purposes. For example, in a query showing the data for only the customers in California, you do not need to display the State field in the results.

TIP

Change the order of fields in a query. *In the design grid, click the column selector for the column you want to move. The column selector is the thin gray box at the top of a column. Use the mouse pointer to drag the selected column to a new position.*

Add a Field to a Query

1 Display the query in Design view.

2 In the field list at the top of the Design view window, double-click a field name to place the field in the next available column in the design grid, or click and drag a field to a specific column in the design grid.

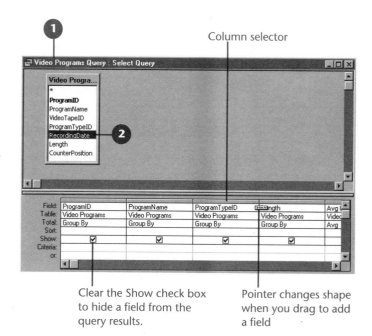

Column selector

Clear the Show check box to hide a field from the query results.

Pointer changes shape when you drag to add a field

Remove a Field from a Query

1 Display the query in Design view.

2 Select the field by clicking its column selector, and then press Delete.

When you remove a field from the query design grid, you're only removing it from the query specifications. You're not deleting the field and its data from the underlying table.

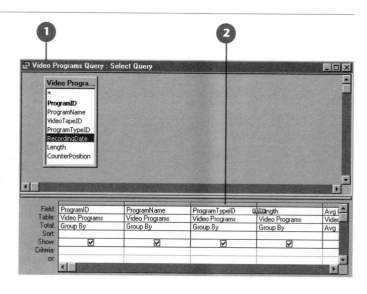

TIP

Remove a table from the design grid. *To remove a table, right-click the table to select it and display the shortcut menu, and then click Remove Table.*

Add a Field from Another Table to a Query

1 Display the query in Design view.

2 Click the Show Table button on the Query Design toolbar.

3 Select the table that contains the fields you want to include in the query.

4 Click Add.

5 Repeat steps 3 and 4 for each table you want to include.

6 Click Close.

7 Double-click or drag the fields you want to include to the design grid.

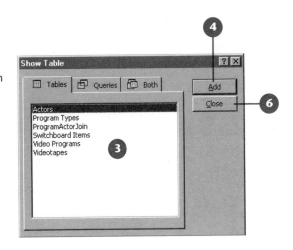

5

Retrieving Only the Records You Want

For each field you include in a query, you can specify criteria that a record must match to be selected when you run the query. For example, you can create a query to retrieve only those records for customers located in a particular city. To view records for customers located in either New York City *or* Boston, you can expand your search with an *OR condition*. You can also narrow your search with an *AND condition*. For example, you could view the records for customers with offices in both New York City *and* Boston; a customer must have offices in both cities to be included in the query results. You can also create a *parameter query* so that the query prompts you to provide specific criteria each time you run the query.

Specify Criteria in a Query

1 Display the query in Design view.

2 Click the Criteria box for the field for which you want to define a selection criterion.

3 Type the first criterion you want for the query.

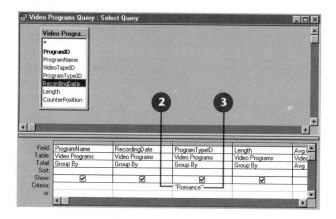

Expand Criteria with an OR Condition

1 Display the query in Design view.

2 In the Criteria row, type the first criteria you want for the query.

3 For each additional OR criteria, enter the criteria in a separate "or" row for the field.

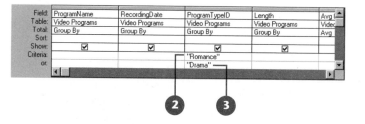

Program Name	Recording Dat	Program Type	Length	Avg Of Length
Killer Frogs	10/8/70	Drama	120	120
Days of Insurrec	12/15/96	Drama	100	100
Caveat Emptor	12/15/96	Drama	110	110
Remembering E	5/4/96	Romance	95	95
More, Much Mo	12/20/96	Romance	95	95
Mea Culpa	7/14/97	Romance	115	115
Krista	7/4/96	Romance	100	100
In the Park	10/21/95	Romance	110	110
Imagining Parac	9/13/96	Romance	115	115
Creating Alexan	1/3/97	Romance	110	110

Record: 1 of 10

The program type field can contain *either* Drama *or* Romance to be included in the query results.

TIP

Specify text to search for in your selection criteria.

When the criterion is a text value, it must be enclosed in quotation marks. Access will insert the quotation marks for you after you type the value and press Tab or Enter.

Restrict Criteria with an AND Condition

1 Display the query in Design view.

2 In the Criteria row, enter the first criteria you want for the query.

3 In the same Criteria row, enter the additional AND criteria for the other field(s) in the query.

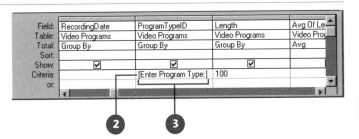

The record must contain both values to be included in the query results.

TIP

Sort the retrieved records.

In Datasheet view, you can select a field and then click the Sort Ascending or Sort Descending button on the Table Datasheet toolbar to sort the query results in either ascending or descending order by the values in the selected field.

SEE ALSO

See "Changing the Order of Records Displayed in a Table" on page 36 for more information about sorting records.

Create a Parameter Query to Prompt You for Criteria

1 Display the query in Design view.

2 Click the Criteria box for the field for which you want to be prompted to enter a value.

3 Type the text of your prompt surrounded by square brackets.

4 Click the Run Button on the Query Design toolbar.

5 Enter criteria information.

6 Click OK.

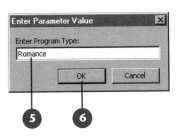

Creating a Query to Summarize Values

A *crosstab query* allows you to summarize the contents of fields that contain numeric values, such as Date fields or Number fields. In this type of query, the results of the summary calculations are shown at the intersection of rows and columns. For example, suppose you wanted to see the average number of times a video was rented based on movie length and movie type. You could create a crosstab query to display the movie type in rows and the movie lengths as column headings. At the intersection of each row and column, you would see the average number of times the movies of that type and length were rented.

Create a Crosstab Query

1 From the Queries tab in the Database window, click New, click Crosstab Query Wizard, and then click OK.

2 From the list at the top of the dialog box, select the table or query that contains the records you want to retrieve, and then click Next.

3 Select the fields for the rows in the Crosstab Query, and then click Next.

4 Select the field for the columns in the Crosstab Query, and then click Next.

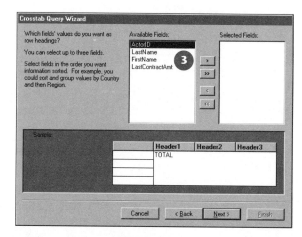

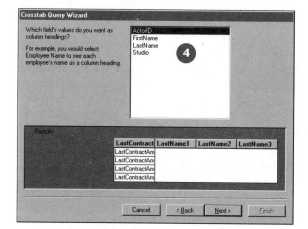

TIP

More about functions. *The list of functions available in the Crosstab Query Wizard dialog box changes depending on the kind of data available in the selected field.*

"What's an easy way to summarize numeric data in my database?"

5 In the Fields box, click the field whose values you want to be calculated and displayed for each row and column intersection.

6 In the Functions box, click the function you want for the calculation to be performed.

7 Click the check box if you want to see a total for each row, or clear the check box if you do not want to see a total for each row.

8 Click Next to display the final Crosstab Query Wizard dialog box.

9 Type a name for your query.

10 Click Finish.

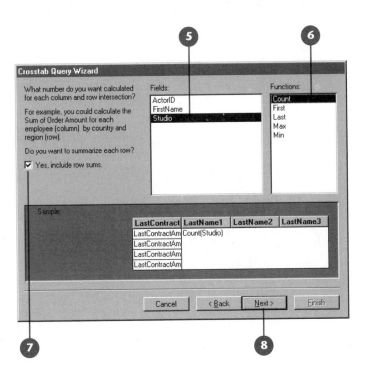

This Crosstab query results show the total number of actors in each studio for a given contract amount.

Detail information shows the contract amount for each actor.

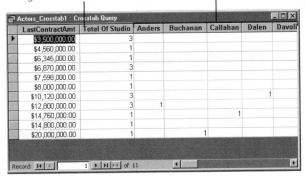

LastContractAmt	Total Of Studio	Anders	Buchanan	Callahan	Dalen	Davoli
$3,500,000.00	3					
$4,560,000.00	1					
$6,345,000.00	1					
$6,870,000.00	3					
$7,598,000.00	1					
$8,000,000.00	1					
$10,120,000.00	3				1	
$12,800,000.00	3	1				
$14,760,000.00	1			1		
$14,800,000.00	1					
$20,000,000.00	1		1			

Record: I◄ ◄ 1 ► ►I ►✱ of 11

Displaying a Query in Design View

After you create a query, you might decide that you want to make some changes to it. For example, you might want to see the information in other fields or enter new selection criteria. Instead of creating a new query, you can simply modify the existing one. To change a query, you need to display the query in Design view, and then modify the query design. Then you can switch back to Datasheet view to see the results of the modified query.

Design View button

Change to Design View from the Database Window

1. In the Database window, select the query whose design you want to see.

2. Click Design.

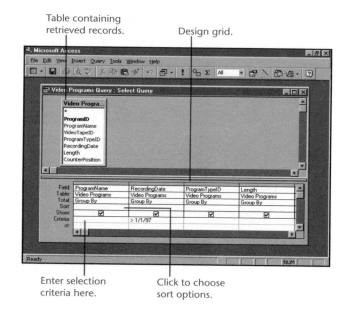

Table containing retrieved records.

Design grid.

Enter selection criteria here.

Click to choose sort options.

Switch Between Design View and Datasheet View

1. In Design view, click the View button on the Query Design toolbar.

2. In Datasheet view, click the View button on the Table Datasheet toolbar.

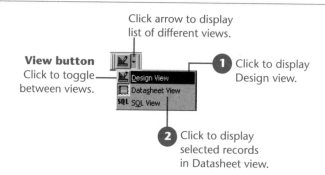

Click arrow to display list of different views.

View button
Click to toggle between views.

1. Click to display Design view.

2. Click to display selected records in Datasheet view.

Putting Queries to Work

Queries are the workhorse of your database. You can use queries not only to retrieve the records you want, but with the aid of the Expression Builder, you can use queries to locate records within a range of values. You can also use the Expression Builder to explicitly exclude certain records.

In addition, you can create action queries. *Action queries* are special queries that can help you add or delete records from a table, maintain a table, and even create new tables in a database. There are four kinds of action queries:

◆ *Append queries* add the records in the query results to a table.

◆ *Make-Table queries* create a table that includes the records in the query results.

◆ *Delete queries* delete from a table the records that are displayed in the query results.

◆ *Update queries* update information for the records displayed in the query results.

Comparing Values in Selection Criteria

The *Expression Builder* allows you to compare values using comparison operators, so that you can include a range of values in your selection criteria. By clicking buttons for the operators you want to use, you use the Expression Builder to further customize your query. For example, you can use comparison operators to select these records within a range of dates. Similarly, you can use logical expressions in your selection criteria to exclude records of a particular type. When you run the query, Access will perform the required comparisons and display the results.

Build button

Insert a Comparison Expression

1 Display the query in Design view.

2 Position the insertion point in the Criteria box for which you want to include an expression.

3 Click the Build button on the Query Design toolbar.

4 Click the appropriate comparison operator button. Or to see additional comparison operators, click the Operators folder, click Comparison, and then choose the comparison operator you want from the list on the right.

5 Enter a value or click a field whose value you want to compare.

6 Click OK.

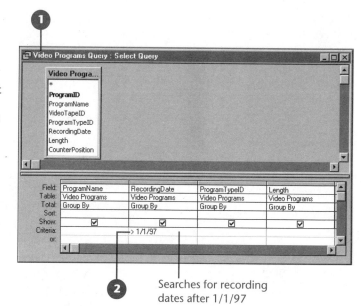

Searches for recording dates after 1/1/97

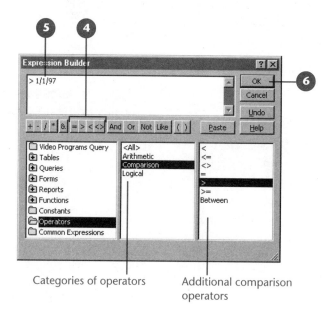

Categories of operators

Additional comparison operators

Include text in your expression. *When entering the contents of a text field (one that does not contain numbers or dates) you must surround the text with quotation marks.*

Fine tune selection criteria. *To further fine tune your selection criteria, combine logical and comparison operators in the same expression.*

Insert a Logical Expression

1 Display the query in Design view.

2 Position the insertion point in the Criteria box for which you want to include an expression.

3 Click the Build button on the Query Design toolbar.

4 Click one of the logical operator buttons. Or to see additional logical operators, click the Operators folder, click Logical, and then choose the logical operator you want from the list on the right.

5 Enter a value or click a field whose value you want to use in the expression.

6 Click OK.

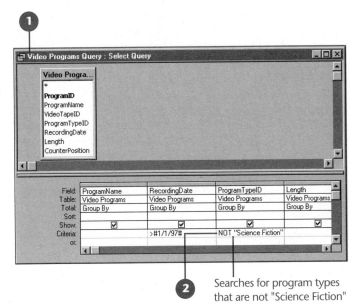

Searches for program types that are not "Science Fiction"

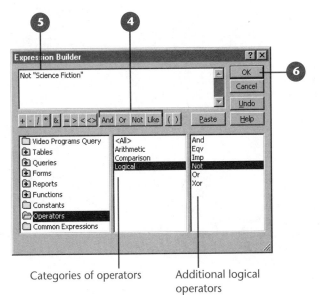

Categories of operators

Additional logical operators

6

Calculating Values in a Query

In addition to the built-in functions you can use to compare values in a query, you can use the *Expression Builder* to create your own calculations using arithmetic operators. By clicking the operator buttons you want to use and entering constant values as needed, you can use the Expression Builder to include expressions in a query. For example, to determine fees based on a contract amount, you can create an arithmetic expression in your query to compute the results. When you run the query, Access performs the required calculations and displays the results.

TIP

Rename a calculated field.
Click the calculated field in the design grid, and then click the Properties button on the Query Design toolbar. Enter a new name in the Caption box, and then click OK.

Create a Calculated Field

1. Display the query in Design view.

2. Position the insertion point in the Field row for a blank column in the design grid.

3. Click the Build button on the Query Design toolbar to display the Expression Builder dialog box.

4. Double-click the field (or fields) you want to use in the calculation.

5. Click the button corresponding to the calculation you want; or click the Operators folder, click the Arithmetic folder, and then click the operator you want to use.

6. Type any other values (constants) you want to include in the expression.

7. Click OK to insert the calculation in the field.

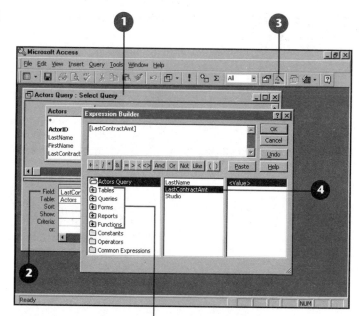

Click to choose fields from another table or other database object.

Place parentheses around the parts of the expression you want calculated first.

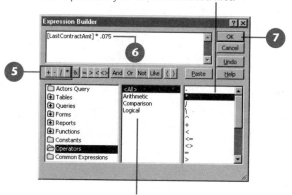

Categories of operators

Changing the Appearance of Values

Sometimes the values that appear in the results of a query might not be formatted the way you want. For example, when Access first calculates an expression in a query, the results appear in the default number format (no commas and values displayed to 6 decimal places). With the Properties feature, you can specify the format in which you want values to appear.

TIP

Change the column heading without changing the field name. *In the Field Properties dialog box, you can enter a new column heading for a field by typing new text in the Caption box. The caption you enter will appear only in the query results; the field name in the table will not change.*

Change a Number Format

1 Position the insertion point in the number field whose format you want to change, and then click the Properties button on the Query Design toolbar.

2 Click the Format drop-down arrow, and then select the format you want to use.

The name of the format appears on the left side of the drop-down list and examples of the corresponding format appear on the right side.

3 Click in the Decimal Places box, and then select one of the available decimal places from the drop-down list, or enter the number of decimal places you want.

4 Click the Close button.

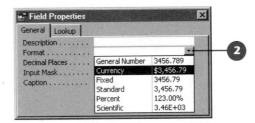

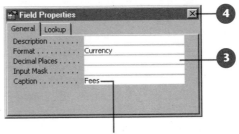

You can type new text for a column heading

The caption property sets the column heading to "Fees."

Last Name	LastContractAmt	Studio	Fees
Fuller	$8,000,000.00	MDI	$600,000.00
Davolio	$6,345,000.00	ScreenWerx	$475,875.00
Leverling	$14,800,000.00	StarMajic	$1,110,000.00
Buchanan	$20,000,000.00	AllStar	$1,500,000.00
Suyama	$10,120,000.00	Panoramic	$759,000.00
Peacock	$7,598,000.00	MasterView	$569,850.00
Callahan	$14,760,000.00	Panoramic	$1,107,000.00
Dodsworth	$12,800,000.00	ScreenWerx	$960,000.00
King	$3,500,000.00	Panoramic	$262,500.00
Labrune	$4,560,000.00	ScreenWerx	$342,000.00
Franken	$6,870,000.00	MasterView	$515,250.00
Snyder	$12,800,000.00	MasterView	$960,000.00

Record: 1 of 19

These values appear in the Currency format.

6

Creating a Query to Add Records

You can use a query to add records to a table by creating an *append query*. The records that appear in the query results are the records that the query will append to the table that you specify. If the fields you've selected have the same name in both tables, Access automatically fills the matching name in the Append To row in the design grid. If the fields in the two tables don't have the same name, enter the names of the fields in the Append To row in the design grid.

TIP

Appending records with a primary key. *If the table you are appending records to includes a primary key field, the records you are appending must have the same field or an equivalent field of the same data type. Access won't append any of the records if either duplicate or empty values would appear in the primary key field.*

Create a Query to Add Records

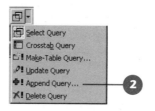

1. Create a simple query based on the table whose records you want to append to another table.

2. In Design view, click the Query Type button drop-down arrow on the Query Design toolbar, and then click Append Query.

3. Type the name of the table to which you want to append records; or click the drop-down arrow and choose a table from the list.

4. Click Current Database if the table is in the currently open database, or click Another Database and type the name of another database (including the path, if necessary).

5. Click OK.

6. Drag the fields you want to append from the field list to the query design grid. If you want to append all fields with the same name as fields in the new table you're appending to, you can drag the asterisk (*) to the query design grid.

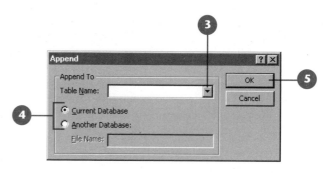

7 If the primary key is not an AutoNumber data type, drag the primary key field from the table to the design grid.

8 Drag from the field list any fields you want to use in selection criteria.

9 Enter the criteria that will determine the records you want to add.

10 To preview the records that will be added, click the View button on the Query Design toolbar. To return to Design view, click the View button on the Table Datasheet toolbar.

11 Click the Run button on the Query Design toolbar to append the records.

12 Click Yes to confirm that you want to append the records.

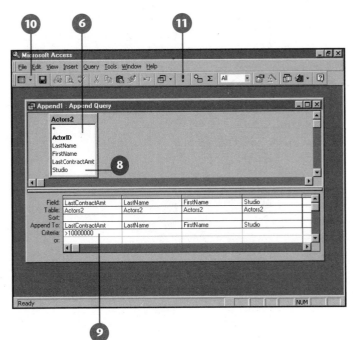

Creating a Query to Create a New Table

You can create a new table from the records that appear in the query results. By using the *Make-Table Query* option you can quickly combine information from multiple tables and make a new table that contains the records retrieved in the query.

Query Type button

Create a Query to Create a New Table

1. Create a query based on the tables or queries that contain the records you want to put in a new table.

2. In Design view, click the Query Type button drop-down arrow on the Query Design toolbar, and then click Make-Table Query.

3. Type the name of the table you want to create; or click the drop-down arrow and choose a table from the list if you want to replace the existing table with a new one.

4. Click Current Database if the table is in the currently open database, or click Another Database and type the name of another database (including the path, if necessary).

5. Click OK.

6. Drag the fields you want in the new table from the field list to the query design grid.

7. Specify the criteria for the fields, if necessary.

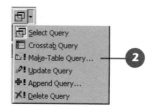

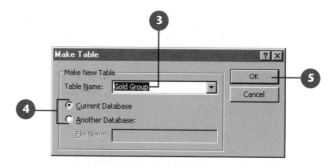

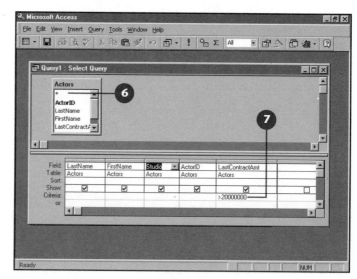

Set the primary key and establish table properties.

After you run a make-table query, you might want to switch to the new table's Design view and set a primary key and table properties. Also it is a good idea to examine and change, as needed, the field properties in the new table because they do not inherit the field properties from the original table.

8 To preview the records that will appear in the new table, click the View button on the Query Design toolbar. To return to Design view, click the View button on the Table Datasheet toolbar.

9 Click the Run button on the Query Design toolbar to make the new table.

10 Click Yes to confirm that you want to create the new table from the query results.

LastName	FirstName	Studio	ActorID	LastContractAmt
Leverling	Janet	StarMajic	3	$20,200,390.00
King	Robert	Panoramic	9	$20,200,390.00
Snyder	Howard	MasterView	12	$20,200,390.00
Martin	Dale	StarMajic	13	$20,200,390.00
Huston	Bucky	AllStars	34	$20,500,390.00
			(AutoNumber)	

Gold Group : Table

Record: 5 of 5

The preview shows that only those records with a LastContractAmt value greater than $20,000,000.00 will be added to the new table.

6

Creating a Query to Delete Records

A *delete query* removes records from the current table. Based on the selection criteria you specify, a delete query deletes the records that appear in the query results. Before the records are deleted, Access displays the retrieved records and prompts you to confirm that you want to delete them.

Create a Query to Delete Records

1. Create a new query based on the table that contains the record(s) you want to delete.

2. In Design view, click the Query Type button drop-down arrow on the Query Design toolbar, and then click Delete Query.

3. For the table from which you want to delete records, drag the asterisk (*) from the field list to the fields query design grid. This indicates that all the fields will be selected for the records you want to delete.

4. Drag one or more fields from the table list to the design grid, and then enter the selection criteria in the Criteria box for each field.

5. To preview the records that will be deleted, click the View button on the Query Design toolbar.

6. Click the Run button on the Query Design toolbar to delete the records.

7. Click Yes to confirm that you want to delete the records.

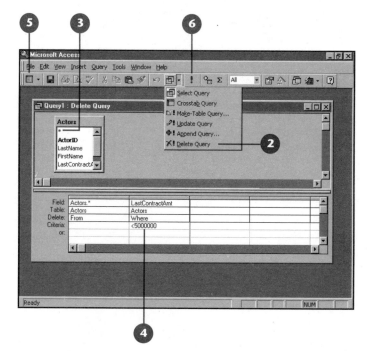

The preview shows that only those records with a LastContractAmt value less than $5,000,000.00 will be deleted.

Creating a Query to Update Records

An *update query* allows you to make changes to all the records in a table or to only specific records that match the criteria that you specify. For example, in a table containing product prices, you could add 10% to all price values in a table. Or you might reduce price values for only those products that have sold a lower than average number of units.

Create a Query to Update Records

1. Create a query based on the tables or queries that include the records you want to update and the fields you want to use for the selection criteria.

2. In Design view, click the Query Type button drop-down arrow on the Query Design toolbar, and then click Update Query.

3. Drag the fields you want to update or for which you want to specify criteria from the field list to the query design grid.

4. Specify the criteria for the fields, if necessary.

5. In the Update To box for the fields you want to update, type the expression or value you want to use to change the fields.

6. To preview the records that will be updated, click the View button on the Query Design toolbar.

7. Click the Run button on the Query Design toolbar to update the records.

8. Click Yes to confirm that you want to update the records.

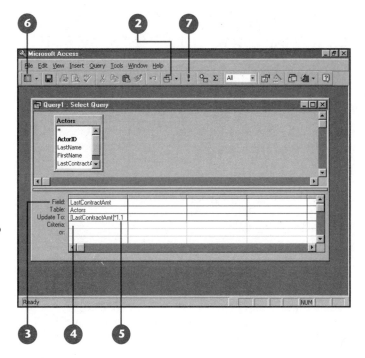

6

Speeding Up Searches with Indexing

Just like an index in a book, an index in Access can find and sort information faster, especially in a very large table. You index fields you frequently search or sort, or fields you join to fields in other tables in queries. Consider indexing if you expect to search or sort by values in the field. If the field contains many different values, (rather than many values that are the same), indexing can significantly speed up queries. After indexing a field, you can view and then modify indexes as necessary.

Create a Field Index

1 Display the table in the Design view, and then click the field (in the top of the table) for which you want to create an index.

2 In the Field Properties section, click the right side of the Indexed property box.

3 From the drop-down list click one of the following:

- ◆ Yes (Duplicates OK) if you want to allow multiple records to have the same data in this field.

- ◆ Yes (No Duplicates) option if you want to ensure that no two records have the same data in this field.

4 Click the Save button on the Table Design toolbar.

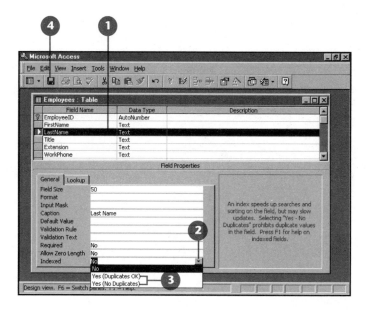

You cannot index all data types. *You do not need to index the primary key of a table, because it is automatically indexed. You can index a field only if the data type is Text, Number, Currency, or Date/Time. You cannot index a field whose data type is Memo or OLE Object.*

View or Edit Indexes

1 Open the table in Design view.

2 Click the Indexes button on the Table Design toolbar.

3 Change indexes or index properties.

4 Click the Indexes button when you have finished viewing or editing the indexes and index properties.

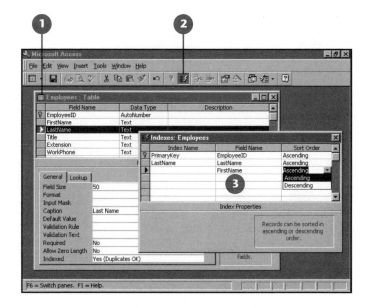

Creating Multiple Field Indexing

If you think you'll often search or sort by two or more fields at a time, you can create a multiple-field index. For example, if you often specify criteria for LastName and FirstName fields in the same query, create a multiple-field index on both fields.

Create a Multiple-Field Index

1 Open the table in Design view.

2 Click the Indexes button on the Table Design toolbar.

3 In the Indexes window, click in the first blank row in the Index Name column and type the name you want for your index.

4 Click the right side of the first blank row in the Field Name column and select a field to include in this index.

5 Click the right side of the next blank row in the Field Name column and select another field to include in this index.

Repeat this step until you have selected all the fields you want to include in the index.

6 Click the Indexes button on the Table Design toolbar when you have finished viewing or editing the indexes and index properties.

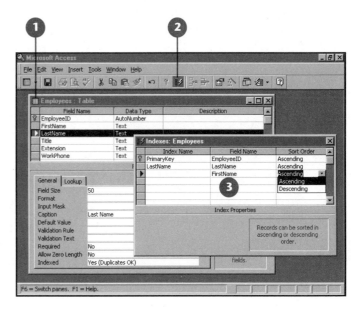

7

Creating a Database

When you need to manage information not already in an existing Microsoft Access 97 database, you can create a new database. Creating a database involves:

◆ Planning the database to determine the kind of information it will contain

◆ Creating the tables

◆ Establishing the necessary relationships between tables

◆ Entering or importing information into the tables

After you have created a database and worked with it for a while, your information needs might change. If so, you can always modify the design of the tables to meet any new information requirements.

71

Planning a Database

Planning a database is an important first step in creating your own database. Although you can always make changes to your database when necessary, a little planning before you begin can save you a lot of time later on. For example, when you create a table in a database, you specify the type of data that will be stored in each field. Although you can change the field type (for example, from text to a number), you would need to reenter all the information for that field for all the records in the table if you change the data type after you have entered data in this field. It's better to plan ahead and anticipate possible uses of your information. Think about the information you need to keep track of, when you need it, and the questions you need to answer using this information. Think about how you currently keep a record of this information and what you would like to do differently. In many respects, creating a new database in Access gives you the opportunity to rethink your information requirements.

Planning Tables

Because a database can contain multiple tables, consider organizing your database information into several tables—each one containing only the fields related to a specific topic—rather than one large table that contains all the fields you need for the entire database. For example, you could create a Customers table that contains only customer information and an Orders table that contains only customer order information.

Establishing Table Relationships

Sometimes you'll want to retrieve data from multiple tables at the same time. For example, you might want to view information from both a Customers table and an Orders table so that you could see which orders were placed by specific customers. In order to retrieve data from multiple tables, you need to establish the necessary relationships between tables through the use of a common field. A *common field* is a field that exists in more than one table so that you can connect the tables. For example, a Customers table might contain a CustomerID field. You could include this same field in an Orders table so that you could connect the two tables. The CustomerID field would be the common field in this relationship.

Other than the common field, take care to avoid creating the same fields in multiple tables. This saves space and reduces errors caused by incorrectly updating the same information in multiple tables.

Specifying a Primary Key

When planning a table, you should also identify the primary key. The *primary key* is one or more fields whose values uniquely identify each record in a table. For example, a Social Security number field in a personnel table would be the primary key, because each employee has a unique Social Security number. Although designating a primary key is not mandatory, doing so is a good idea because the primary key facilitates sorting and locating the data you want to see.

Assigning a primary key to a table also facilitates establishing relationships between tables

When you use the primary key as the common field to establish a relationship between two tables, it is called the *foreign key* in the second table. In the previous example, the CustomerID field would be the primary key in the Customers table and a foreign key in the Orders table.

Choosing How to Create a Database

As with most other objects you create in Access, you can create a new database file using one of the Database Wizards or you can use the Blank Database option to create and name a database file. A Database Wizard guides you through the process of naming a new database file and specifying the tables for your database. For each table, you can indicate the fields it should contain. Using a wizard you can choose from several types of tables and fields, including customer and contact information tables. If you create a blank database, you must name the database file and then start creating new tables from the Database window.

New Database button
If Access is already open, click to create a new database using a wizard (or a blank database).

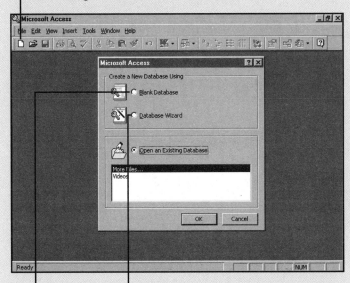

Click to create a new blank database.

Click to create a new database using a wizard.

Creating a Database with a Wizard

Access provides a variety of Database Wizards you can use to create databases that are suitable for different business or personal information needs. Each wizard guides you through the process of creating all the tables you need to create a database that you can begin using right away. These wizards also create useful queries, reports, and forms that will make it easier to use the database. You can even have Access supply data in the tables so you can see the database in action.

Create a Database with a Wizard

1. Start Access, click the Database Wizard option button, and then click OK. Or, if Access is already open, click the New Database button on the Database toolbar.

2. Click the Databases tab and double-click the wizard for the kind of database you want to create.

3. Click the Save In drop-down arrow, and then select the drive and the folder in which you want to store your database file.

4. In the File Name text box, type a filename for the database, or use the default filename. A database filename can contain up to 255 characters, including spaces, numbers, and symbols. When you type a filename, you can use both uppercase and lowercase letters.

5. Click Create.

Types of databases you can create with a wizard.

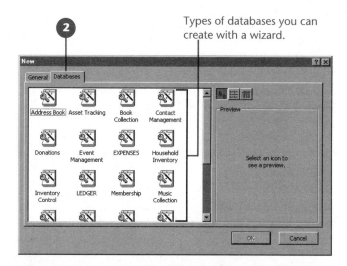

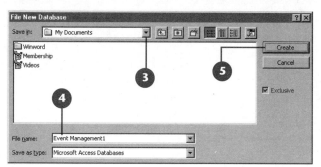

6 The first Database Wizard dialog box identifies the kind of information that you will be able to store in your new database. Each item corresponds to a table that you will create with the wizard. Click Next to continue.

7 On the left side of the dialog box, select a table.

8 Click the check box for each optional (unchecked) field you also want to include. If you change your mind, you can clear the check box for any optional field you want to exclude. Click Next to continue.

9 Click a style for the forms in the database, and then click Next to continue.

10 Click a style for the reports in the database, and then click Next to continue.

11 Type a name for your database (this name can be different from the database filename). Click Next to continue.

12 Indicate whether or not you want to start the new database right away. Click Finish to have Access build the database according to your selections.

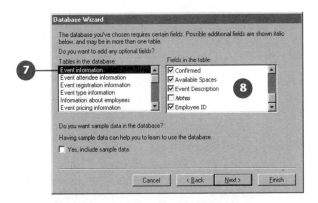

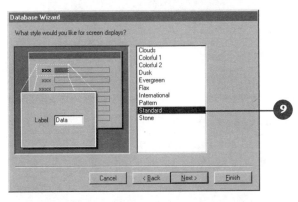

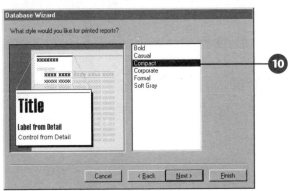

Creating Tables in a Database

After creating a database file, you need to create the tables in the database. You can also create additional tables in an existing database. There are several ways to create a new table: in Design view, in Datasheet view, with a Table Wizard, or by importing data from another program, such as Microsoft Excel. Depending on the method you choose, creating a table can involve one or more of the following:

♦ Specifying the fields for the table

♦ Determining the data type for each field

♦ Determining the field size (for text and number fields only)

♦ Assigning the primary key

♦ Saving and naming the table

METHODS FOR CREATING A TABLE	
Method	**Description**
Design	In Design view, you must specify the fields, specify the data type for each field, assign the size (for text view and number fields), assign the primary key, and save the table yourself.
Datasheet	When you create a table in Datasheet view, you can start viewing and entering data right away. Access automatically assigns the field type based on the kind of information you entered in the field, and it assigns a default field size for text and number fields. After you close and save the table, Access prompts you to identify a primary key or Access will designate one for you.
Table Wizard	Using a Table Wizard, you select fields from sample tables that are appropriate for the type of database you are creating. The data type and other field properties are already defined for each field.
Importing a Table	When you import a table, all the field names and data types are retained with the imported data. However, you must name the new table and identify the primary key or have Access create a primary key for you. Also, you might need to change the field size and other properties after importing.
Linking a table	When you link a table, the table data is retrieved from a table in another database. Linking a table saves disk space because there is only one table rather than multiple tables with the same data. Linking a table saves time because there is no need to update the same information in more than one table.

Working in Design View

Primary Key button
Click to assign or remove the
primary key designation for a field.

Insert Rows button
Click to add new fields
to the table.

Delete Rows button
Click to remove selected
fields from the table.

Click to switch to
Datasheet view.

Click to specify
a data type.

Type a description
of the field here
(optional).

Field properties

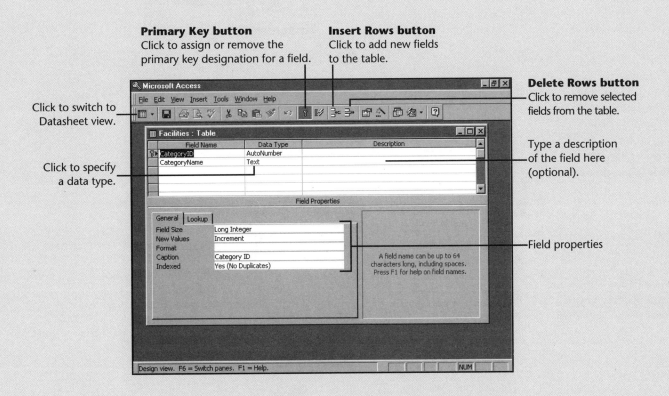

Creating Tables the Easy Way

One of the easiest ways to create a table is to use the Table Wizard. The *Table Wizard* displays a series of dialog boxes in which you can enter selections for your table. You choose from a number of tables suitable for a variety of databases and select the fields that you want to use. You can also rename the fields to what makes sense for you. With the wizard you also indicate any relationship between the new table and other tables in the database (if any), and you identify the primary key or have Access assign one for you.

Start the Table Wizard

1 On the Tables tab of the Database window, click New and then double-click Table Wizard.

2 Click the Business or Personal option button.

3 Choose the table that best matches your needs.

4 In the Sample Fields list, double-click each field you want to include in the table to copy the selected field to the Fields In My New Table list.

5 Click Next to continue.

6 Type a new name for the table or accept the suggested name.

7 Click the first option button to have the Table Wizard assign the primary key, or click the second option button to assign your own primary key. Click Next to continue. If you choose to assign your own primary key, you will see another dialog box describing primary key options. After you specify your primary key preferences, click OK to return to the Table Wizard.

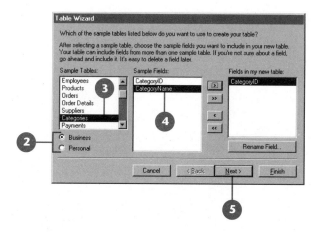

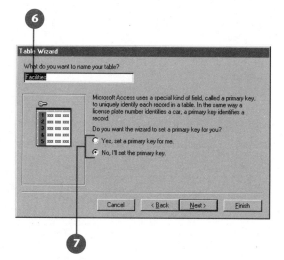

SEE ALSO

See "Assigning a Primary Key" on page 80 for information about the primary key field.

SEE ALSO

See "Defining Table Relationships" on page 198 for information on relating tables to one another.

8 Review the relationships of this new table with the other tables in the database. If you want to make any changes to the relationships, select the relationship you want to change, click the Relationships button, specify the new table relationships, and click OK; then click Next to continue.

9 Indicate whether you want to start entering data right away (either in Datasheet view or in a form that Access creates for you) or whether you want to see the table's design in Design view.

10 Click Finish to complete the wizard and create the table.

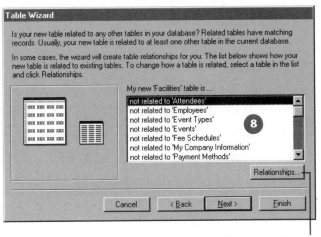

Click to specify table relationships

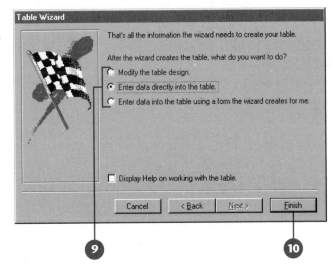

Assigning a Primary Key

In the Table Wizard, you have the option to assign your own primary key (rather than having the Table Wizard do it for you). You can also assign or change the primary key in Design view. In either case, the primary field must contain information that is unique to each record in this table. For example, do not use the PostalCode field (or Zip Code field) as a primary key field because it is likely that several records in your table would have the same zip code. On the other hand, a customer ID number or Social Security number would be a good choice, because these numbers are different for each record.

Specifying a Primary Key Field in Design View

In Design view, you can use the Primary Key button to assign or remove the primary key designation for the selected field. When you use the Table Wizard to assign a primary key field, you identify the type of numbering you want to use for the primary key field. The adjacent table describes the data type numbering options.

Primary key field

Primary Key button
Click to assign or remove a primary key.

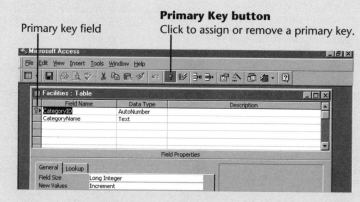

PRIMARY DATA TYPE NUMBERING OPTIONS

Option	Description	Field Type
Consecutive numbers Access assigns automatically to new records	As you enter each new record, Access automatically numbers each record consecutively. You cannot enter or edit data in an AutoNum field.	AutoNum
Number I enter when I add new records	When you enter a record, you type a unique number that identifies the record. Choose this option if the field will contain Social Security numbers or other identification numbers. You cannot enter letters in this field when entering records.	Number
Numbers and/ or letters I enter when I add new records	When you enter a record, you type a unique number that identifies this record. Choose this option if the field will contain letters as well as numbers.	Text

Assigning Table Relationships in the Table Wizard

When you create a table using the Table Wizard, you have the option to relate the new table to another table or tables in the database. Of the different types of relationships you can create, the most common is the *one-to-many relationship*. Each record in the first table (the primary table) is related to zero, one, or many records in the second table (the related table). For example, because only one customer places an order, but each customer can place many orders, a one-to-many relationship would apply if a Customers table was the primary table and an Orders table was the related table. If you want to change the table relationship later, you can adjust table relationships in Design view.

SEE ALSO

See "Defining Table Relationships" on page 198 for more information about establishing table relationships.

Create a One-To-Many Relationship

1. Start the Table Wizard and make selections according to your preferences for the table.

2. Click the Next button to proceed through the Table Wizard after you make each selection.

3. In the appropriate dialog box, select the table whose relationship you want to change.

4. Click the Relationships button.

5. Click the middle option button to make the new table the primary table and the selected table the related table, or click the last option button to make the selected table the primary table and the new table the related table.

6. Click OK.

7. Select another table whose relationship you want to change, and then repeat steps 3 through 6.

8. When you have finished specifying table relationships, return to the Table Wizard and complete the Table Wizard.

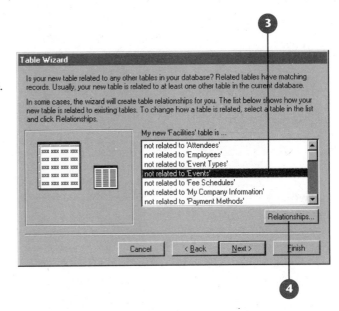

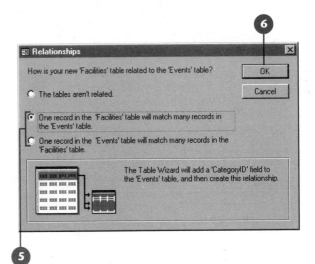

Displaying a Table in Design View

When you display a table in Design view, you can modify the characteristics of the table. For example you can add and delete fields, change the order of fields, change field properties, change the data type, and modify other field characteristics to customize your table. After you make your changes in Design view, you can click the View button on the toolbar to switch to Datasheet view and enter records. If you need to return to Design view, click the View button again. Notice that the icon displayed on the View button changes as you switch between views.

View button

Display a Table in Design View from the Database Window

1 In the Database window, click the Tables tab.

2 Click the table you want to view.

3 Click Design.

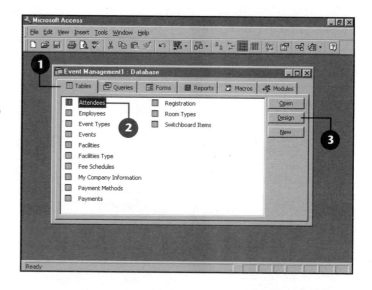

Switching Between Design and Views Datasheet

1 In either Design view or Datasheet view, click the View button drop-down arrow on the toolbar to display the table in the other view.

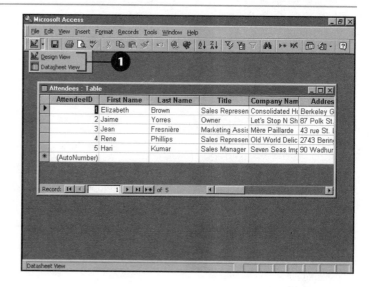

Specifying Data Types

7

A *data type* is a characteristic you assign a field when you are specifying fields for your table. The data type you choose determines the kind of information you can enter in a field. Selecting the appropriate data type makes it easier for you to enter and retrieve information in your tables.

You can always change the data type for a field even after you have entered data in it. However, you might need to perform a potentially lengthy process of converting or retyping the field's data when you save the table. If the data type in a field conflicts with a new data type setting, you may lose some or all of the data in the field. You can use the Format property in the Properties dialog box to specify a format for many of the data types.

Click to display the data types for a field.

DATA TYPES	
Setting	**Type of Data**
Text (default)	Text or combinations of text and numbers, as well as numbers that don't require calculations, such as phone numbers.
Memo	Lengthy text or combinations of text and numbers.
Number	Numeric data used in mathematical calculations.
Date/Time	Date and time values for the years 100 through 9999.
Currency	Currency values and numeric data used in mathematical calculations involving data with one to four decimal places. Accurate to 15 digits on the left side of the decimal separator.
AutoNumber	A unique sequential (incremented by 1) number or random number assigned by Access whenever you add a new record to a table. AutoNumber fields can't be updated.
Yes/No	Yes and No values and fields that contain only one of two values (True/False, On/Off).
OLE Object	An object (such as a Microsoft Excel spreadsheet), linked to or embedded in an Access table.
Hyperlink	An instant connection to information on the World Wide Web. By specifying this data type, you can specify a web site as data in this field.
Lookup Wizard	Creates a field that allows you to choose a value from another table or from a list of values using a combo box.

Adding, Deleting, and Changing the Order of Fields

In Design view, you can add new fields to your table. You add a field by inserting a row, entering the field name, and specifying its data type and other properties. If your table includes a field you no longer need, you can delete the field—and any data you might have already entered in the table for this field. You can also change the order of the fields in Design view.

TIP

Enter a description. *The description for a field is optional. The information you enter in the Description column for a field will appear in the status bar when the table is displayed in Datasheet view and the field is current. A good use of the description is to provide data entry instructions. For example, in a Yes/No field you might include an explanation informing the user that "y" and "n" are the only two entries allowed for the field.*

Add a New Field

1 Display the table in Design view.

2 Click the row selector for the field that will be below the new field you want to insert.

3 Click the Insert Rows button on the Table Design toolbar. A new blank row appears above the row you selected.

4 In the Field Name column, type the name of the new field. A field name can contain up to 255 characters (including letters and numbers).

5 Press Tab to move to the Data Type column.

6 Click the drop-down arrow and specify the data type you want to assign to the field, or press Tab to accept the default Text data type.

7 Press Tab to move to the Description column.

8 Type a brief description (optional) of the kind of information this field can contain or include data entry instructions.

9 Set any additional properties for the field. For text and number fields, assign a Field Size (or accept the default size provided).

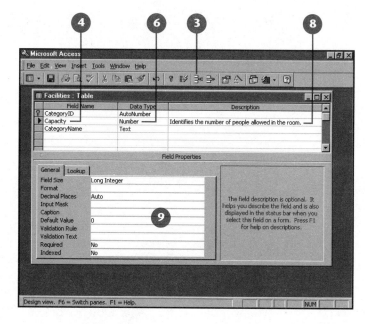

Delete Row button

Delete a Field

1 Display the table in Design view.

2 Click the row selector for the row you want to delete.

3 Click the Delete Rows button on the Table Design toolbar.

4 If any records in the table contain data for this field, you will see a message informing you that deleting this row will also delete data. Click Yes to confirm you want to continue, or click No if you decide not to delete the row and data.

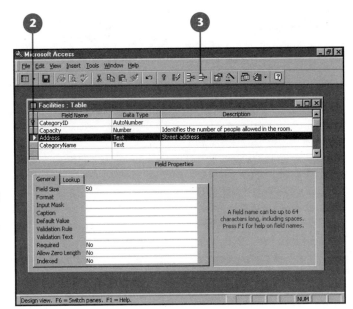

Change the Order of Fields in a Table

1 Display the table in Design view.

2 Click the row selector for the field you want to move. Clicking the row selector selects the field.

3 Click the row selector again and hold down the mouse button to display the move pointer.

4 With the move pointer, drag the row to the new position where you want the field to appear.

The dark line indicates the new position of the row.

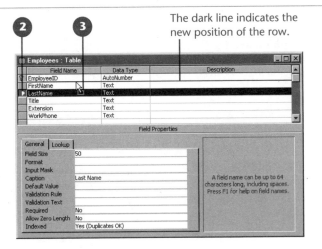

Creating a Custom Table

Although the Table Wizard provides a great head start when creating a new table, sometimes the resulting table doesn't quite meet your needs for information. In that event, it might be faster to create a table from scratch, rather than start from a sample table and make a lot of changes. You can create a new table in Datasheet view or in Design view.

TIP

Specify a data type. *Access examines the data you have entered and determines the correct data type. If you decide to change the data type, switch to Design view and specify a new data type.*

Create a New Table in Datasheet View

1 Click the New button on the Tables tab in the Database window.

2 Click Datasheet View.

3 Click OK.

4 For each field you want to include in the table, double-click one of the default field names (Field1, Field2, etc.), type the name you want for the field, and then press Enter.

5 Enter your data in the datasheet.

6 Click the Save button on the Table Datasheet toolbar.

7 Type a name for the table, and then click OK. Access prompts you to specify a primary key for the table.

8 Click Yes to assign a primary key; then display the table in Design view, select the field you want as the primary key, and then click the Primary Key button on the Table Design toolbar. Or click No if you do not want to assign a primary key at this time.

9 To change any field properties, switch to Design view and make the necessary changes.

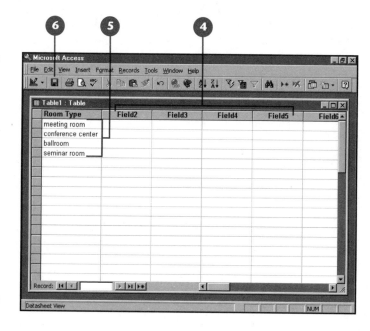

SEE ALSO

See "Specifying Data Types" on page 83 for information about characteristics you want to assign to a field.

SEE ALSO

See "Setting Field Properties" on page 88 for information about formatting fields.

SEE ALSO

See "Assigning a Primary Key" on page 80 for information about the primary key field.

Create a New Table in Design View

1. Click the New button on the Tables tab in the Database window.

2. Click Design View, and then click OK.

3. In the Field Name column, type the name of the first field in the table, and then press Tab.

4. Press Tab to accept the default data type (Text), or click the Data Type drop-down arrow, and then click the data type you want.

5. Press Tab and then type a description (optional).

6. Set any additional properties for the field.

7. Repeat steps 3 through 6 for each field you want to include in your table.

8. Click the Save button on the Table Design toolbar.

9. Type a name for the table and then click OK. Access prompts you to specify a primary key for the table.

10. Click Yes to assign a primary key, select the field you want as the primary key, and then click the Primary Key button on the Table Design toolbar.

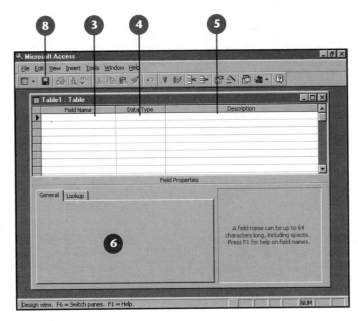

Setting Field Properties

In addition to selecting the data type for a field, you can also set field properties. To some extent field properties are determined by the field data type, but here is a summary of some of the properties you can set for a field:

- Assign a field size (for text and number fields).

- Require data when entering a record, so that no important fields are omitted.

- Set a format for displaying data, so that all records are entered consistently.

- Set rules for accepting (or rejecting) data to assure data it is entered correctly.

- Display a default value (to speed data entry).

- Change the caption property for a field to display a more descriptive name as a column heading.

Set the Format Property

1 Display the table in Design view.

2 Select the field whose Format property you want to change.

3 In the Field Properties section, click the right side of the Format box, and then select the format you want to use.

Depending on the data type for a field, you have a variety of format options, including preset formats for the most common types of formatting for dates, numbers, currency, and yes/no fields.

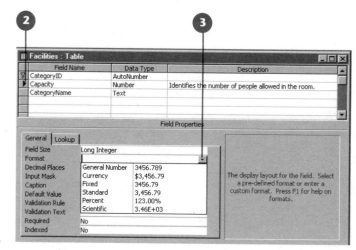

Set the Caption Property

1 Display the table in Design view.

2 Select the field whose Caption property you want to change.

3 In the Field Properties section, select the current text in the Caption box.

4 Type the text you want to appear for the field (column heading) in Datasheet view.

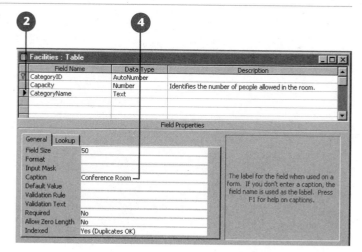

Maintaining Database Information

Entering and maintaining information in the tables in your Microsoft Access 97 database can be labor-intensive activities. Because your database is only as good as the information you store in it, Access has a variety of features that make it easy to enter and maintain data. For example, when entering a number of similar records, you can use the Clipboard to copy and paste records. You can insert information from other Microsoft programs, including pictures, clip art, documents, even hyperlinks to a web site on the Internet.

Not only must you take care to enter the correct information, but you also need to maintain the information to make sure it is accurate and up-to-date. For example, you might need to edit existing data or delete it. You can also check the spelling in your records using the Spelling feature and correct typing mistakes as you work using AutoCorrect.

Entering Records in a Table

There are two ways to enter records in a table. You can enter information in Datasheet view or in a form. If you have just created a new blank table with the Table Wizard, you can enter records using the form that the wizard created for you. If you did not choose to have the wizard create a form, or if no form is available for your table, you can display the table in Datasheet view and enter records in the datasheet's rows. Access automatically saves each record you enter in a table.

TIP

Move to the blank row for entering records. *Click the New Record button on the Table Datasheet toolbar.*

Enter Records in Datasheet View

1 Open the database containing the table in which you want to enter records.

2 In the Database window, click the Tables tab to display the list of tables in the database.

3 Double-click the table in which you want to enter records. The table appears in Datasheet view. The field names appear in columns across the top of the datasheet. The existing records appear in rows.

4 In each field, type the data you want the field to contain. Press Tab or Enter to move to the next field. If the insertion point is in the last field of the record, pressing Tab creates a new record.

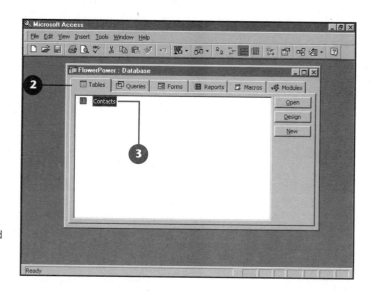

Indicates record you are editing   Click to add a new record

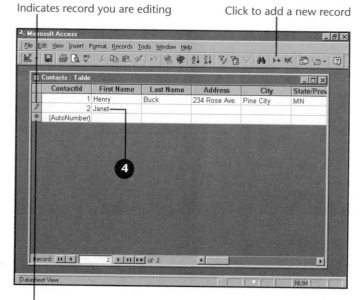

Identifies the next row available for new record

8

TIP

Enter a new record in a form. *If the form already contains data, click the New Record button at the bottom of the form, and enter data in the blank fields.*

TIP

If you hear a beep. *If you hear a beep or tone after entering data, it means that you have made an entry error. A common error is to enter a data type that does not match the data type of the field. For example, if you enter text in a number field, you will hear a beep, and the status bar will display a brief description of the error.*

TIP

Move to a previous field. *You can press Shift+Tab to move to the previous field.*

Enter Records Using a Form

1. Open the database containing the table in which you want to enter records.

2. In the Database window, click the Forms tab to display the list of forms in the database.

3. Double-click the form you want to use to enter records. The first record (if any) in the table appears in the form.

4. In each field, type the data you want the field to contain. Press Tab or Enter to move to the next field. You can press Shift+Tab to move to the previous field or simply click the mouse in the field in which you want to work.

5. Press the Next Record button or Previous button to move to different records.

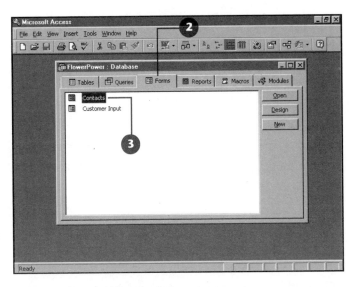

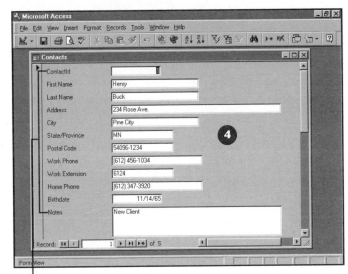

All the fields for the current record are displayed one below the other in a form.

Removing Records

If you no longer want a record included in your table, you can delete it. After you delete a record, you cannot reverse the change with the Undo button, so Access asks you to confirm that you want to delete the record. You can delete one or more selected records in Datasheet view, or you can delete the current record in Form view.

Delete Record button

Delete a Record in Datasheet View

1 Click the row selector for the record you want to delete.

2 Click the Delete Record button on the Table Datasheet toolbar. Access asks you to confirm that you want to delete this record.

3 Click Yes if you want to delete the record, or click No to restore the record to the table.

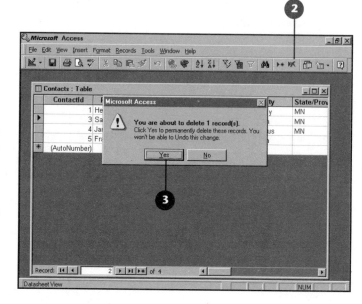

TIP

Delete multiple records. *In Datasheet view, you can delete multiple records at the same time by selecting the records first. Click the row selector for the first record you want to delete, and then drag to select additional rows. Then press Delete to remove all selected records from the table.*

Delete a Record in Form View

1. Display the table in Form view and display the record you want to delete.

2. Click the Delete Record button on the Form View toolbar. Access asks you to confirm that you want to delete this record.

3. Click Yes if you want to delete the record, or click No to restore the record to the table.

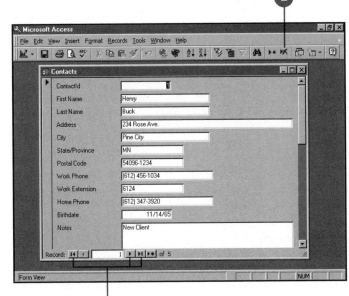

Use the navigation buttons to display the record to be deleted.

Copying and Pasting Records

When you are entering a lot of records in Datasheet view that are nearly identical, you can use the Clipboard to copy and paste existing records to create new records quickly. The *Clipboard* is a temporary area in memory where you can place text you want to reuse or move to another location. After copying and pasting, you can edit individual records to make a few changes. If only part of the record is similar, you can still use the Clipboard to copy and paste a field within the same record or in a new record. To place the text that you want to copy on the Clipboard, you must first select the text, and then copy or cut it. In Access, you can select either the entire record or a single field; you cannot select two fields.

Copy and Paste a New Record

1. In Datasheet view, click the row selector for the row you want to copy.

2. Click the Copy button on the Table Datasheet toolbar.

3. Click the row selector for the new record row.

4. Click the Paste button on the Table Datasheet toolbar. Edit the new record as required.

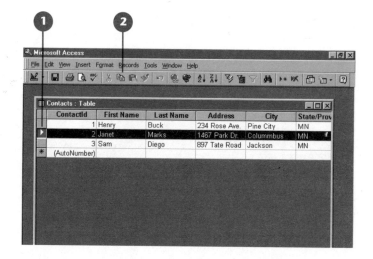

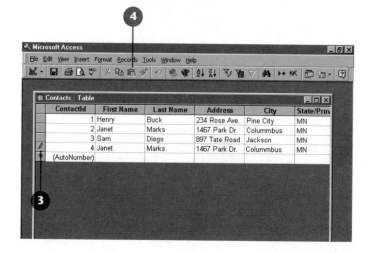

Paste a record between existing records. *If you are pasting within existing rows, click the row selector for the row above which you want to paste the new record.*

Copy and Paste Text

1 In Datasheet view, click the insertion point next to the text you want to copy. Drag to highlight all the text you want to copy.

2 Click the Copy button on the Table Datasheet toolbar.

3 Click in the location where you want to place the text you copied. If you want the contents of the Clipboard to replace existing text, select the existing text before continuing to the next step.

4 Click the Paste button on the Table Datasheet toolbar.

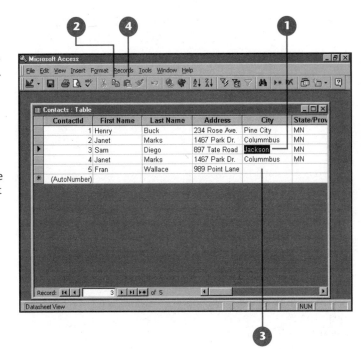

Entering Data More Accurately with AutoCorrect

As you enter data in tables, you might occasionally make typing mistakes. For certain errors, Access will correct the errors as soon as you type them and then press the spacebar or the Enter key. For example, if you type "c o m a p n y" when you mean to type "company," the AutoCorrect feature will correct the error automatically. AutoCorrect fixes typing errors for hundreds of commonly mistyped words. You can also create your own AutoCorrect entries for words or phrases for which you frequently make typing errors.

SEE ALSO

See "Checking Your Spelling" on page 100 for more information about correcting spelling errors.

Replace Text as You Type

◆ To correct incorrect capitalization or spelling errors automatically, continue typing until AutoCorrect makes the required correction.

EXAMPLES OF AUTOCORRECT CHANGES		
Type of Correction	If You Type	AutoCorrect Inserts
Capitalization	ann marie	Ann Marie
Capitalization	microsoft	Microsoft
Capitalization	thursday	Thursday
Common typos	accomodate	accommodate
Common typos	can;t	can't
Common typos	windoes	windows

TIP

Create exceptions to AutoCorrect. *You can also specify abbreviations and terms that you don't want AutoCorrect to automatically correct by clicking the Exceptions button and adding these items to the list of exceptions.*

TIP

Add AutoCorrect entries with the Spelling feature. *Select the misspelled word or abbreviation you want to add as an AutoCorrect entry, and then click the Spelling button. In the Change To box, type the correct word or complete phrase, and then click the AutoCorrect button.*

Add an AutoCorrect Entry

1 Select a word or phrase for which you want to create an AutoCorrect entry.

2 Click the Copy button on the toolbar.

3 Click the Tools menu, and then click AutoCorrect.

4 With the flashing insertion point in the Replace box, press Ctrl+V. Pressing this keyboard shortcut is the same as clicking the Paste button on the toolbar. Because the dialog box is open, you are not able to click the button, so you must use the keyboard shortcut instead.

5 In the With box, type the correct spelling of the text.

6 Click Add.

7 Click OK.

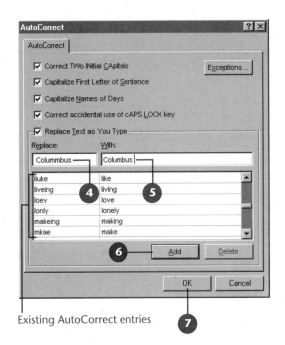

Existing AutoCorrect entries

8

Editing Text in Records

You can edit text you enter in a record. You can select the text you want to change, and then type over it to replace it or press the Delete key to remove it. You can also delete one character at a time. To insert text in a field, place the insertion point in a field and just start typing.

Delete Selected Text in a Field

1 Position the insertion point to the left of the text you want to delete.

2 Drag across the text to highlight it.

You can also double-click a word to select it.

3 Type new text or press Delete to remove the selected text.

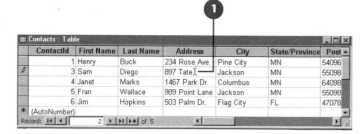

Insert Text in a Field

1 Position the insertion point where you want to insert text.

2 Type the text.

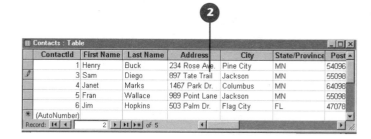

Moving Text

Moving text is similar to copying text, except that you use the Cut button to place the text on the Clipboard (instead of the Copy button). When you click the Cut button, the selected text is removed from the table and placed on the Clipboard.

TIP

The Delete key is not the same as the Cut button.

Although pressing Delete and clicking the Cut button both remove selected text, the Cut button places the selection on the Clipboard, while the Delete key only removes the selection.

Move Text

1 In Datasheet view, click the insertion point next to the text you want to move.

2 Drag to highlight all the text you want to move.

You can double-click a word to select it.

3 Click the Cut button on the Table Datasheet toolbar.

This button removes the selected text from the table and places it on the Clipboard.

4 Click in the location where you want to place the text that you cut.

If you want the contents of the Clipboard to replace existing text, select the existing text before continuing to the next step.

5 Click the Paste button on the table Datasheet toolbar.

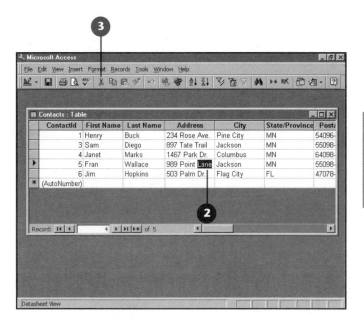

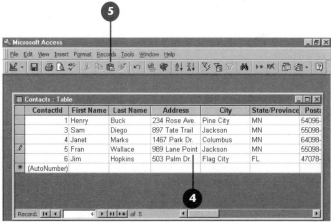

Checking Your Spelling

When you want to verify that the spelling in a field or record is correct, you can use the *Spelling* feature. This feature identifies potentially misspelled words and suggests possible spellings to use instead. You also have the option to correct the spelling, ignore the word, add the word to the dictionary, or create an AutoCorrect entry. In addition, you can control the kinds of spelling errors Access identifies by specifying the spelling options you want in effect.

TIP
Check the spelling in an entire table without opening it. *Click the Tables tab in the Database window, and then select the table you want to check. Click the Spelling button on the Database toolbar.*

Check the Spelling in a Table

1 In Datasheet view, click the row selector for the record whose spelling you want to check or select the field you want to check. Drag to select additional rows. In Form view, you can check the spelling in only a single record at a time.

2 Click the Spelling button on the toolbar. If Access identifies any potentially misspelled words, it opens the Spelling dialog box.

3 Correct or ignore the identified words, as appropriate.

Click to ignore words in this field

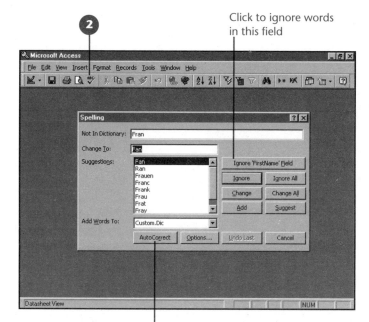

Click to create an AutoCorrect entry

Spelling button

Customize the Spelling dictionary. *Although the Spelling feature provides an extensive dictionary of words to check your spelling against, you can add words to the Custom dictionary. For example, proper names that you frequently use might not be in the dictionary and would be identified as misspelled each time you check the spelling in your table. If you add these special words to the Custom dictionary, the Spelling feature will no longer identify them as misspelled. You can add a word to the Custom dictionary by clicking the Add button in the Spelling dialog box.*

Customize Spelling Options

1 Click the Spelling button on the toolbar.

2 Click Options.

3 Make the selections you want to modify the kinds of spelling errors the Spelling feature will identify.

◆ Clear the Always Suggest option if you do not want the Spelling feature to display a list of suggested spellings.

◆ Clear the From Main Dictionary Only option if you want the Spelling feature to check spelling against the Custom dictionary as well as the Main dictionary. With this option checked (the default setting), the Spelling feature checks spelling against only the Main dictionary.

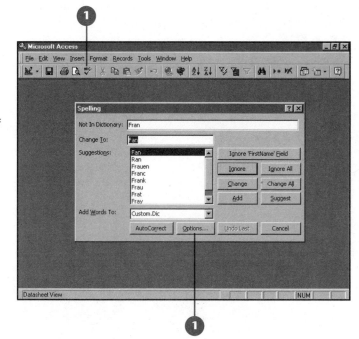

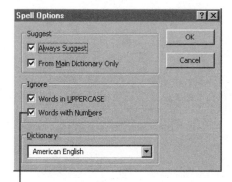

Ignores words that contains numbers (such as license plate numbers).

Getting Data from Other Programs

When you *import* data, you insert a copy of one file into another (in this case Access). Access then creates a new table to store the data, using labels from the first row of a worksheet or table for the new table. You use Access commands to edit the imported data. *Linking* displays information stored in one document (the *source file*) into another (the *destination file*). You can edit the linked object from either file, although changes are stored in the source file.

Import Data from Another Source

1 Open the database into which you want to import data, click the File menu, point to Get External Data, and then click Import.

2 Click the Files Of Type drop-down arrow, and then click the option for the type of file you are importing.

3 If necessary, click the Look In drop-down arrow, and then select the drive and folder that contain the file you want to import.

4 Double-click the name of the file you want to import.

5 If necessary, follow the instructions in the Import Spreadsheet Wizard dialog box to set up Excel data as an Access table.

6 Edit the imported information with Access commands and features.

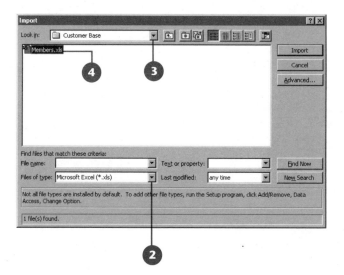

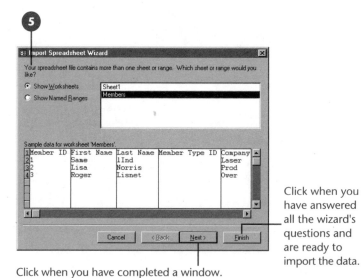

Click when you have answered all the wizard's questions and are ready to import the data.

Click when you have completed a window.

Link Data from Another Source

1 Open the database into which you want to link data, click the File menu, point to Get External Data, and then click Link Tables.

2 Click the Files Of Type drop-down arrow, and then click the option for the type of file you are importing.

3 If necessary, click the Look In drop-down arrow, and then select the drive and folder that contain the file you want to link.

4 Double-click the name of the file you want to link.

5 If necessary, follow the instructions in the Link Spreadsheet Wizard dialog box to set up Excel data as an Access table.

6 From within the source or destination program, edit the linked information using the source program's commands.

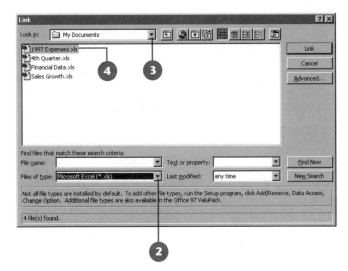

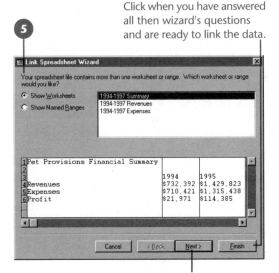

Click when you have answered all then wizard's questions and are ready to link the data.

Click when you have completed a window.

Exporting Data to Other Programs

When you *export* Access data, you save a database object in a new format so that it can be opened in a different program. For example, you might export a table to an Excel worksheet. Or you might want to save your database as an earlier version of Access so someone who hasn't yet upgraded to Access 97 can edit, format, and print it. You can also attach any database object to an e-mail message as an Excel (.xls), Rich Text Format (.rtf), or HyperText Markup Language (.html) file.

Export an Object to Another Program

1. Open the database containing the object you want to export, click the File menu, and then click Save As/Export.

2. Click the To An External File Or Database option button.

3. Click OK.

4. If necessary, click the Save In drop-down arrow, and then select the drive and folder where you want to save the file.

5. Click the Save As Type drop-down arrow, and then click the type of file you want to save the object as.

6. If necessary, type a new name for the file.

7. Click Export.

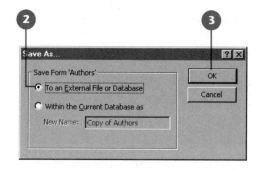

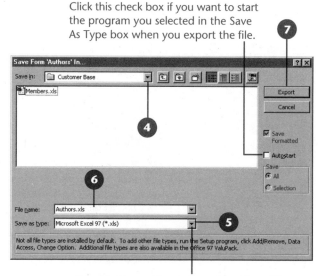

Click this check box if you want to start the program you selected in the Save As Type box when you export the file.

You might want to save an object in a different version of Access or as another database type so another user can edit, format, and print the file.

Attach a Database Object to an E-mail Message

1 In the Database window, click the object you want to attach to an e-mail message.

2 Click the File menu, and then click Send.

3 Double-click the file format you want.

4 Log into your e-mail system if necessary, and then type your message. Access attaches the object to the message in the format you selected.

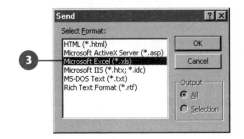

Merging Data with Word

Access is a powerful tool for storing and categorizing large amounts of information. You can combine, or *merge*, database records with Word documents to create tables or produce form letters and envelopes containing names, addresses, and other Access data. For example, you might create a form letter in Word and use an existing Access database with names and addresses to personalize the letters.

OfficeLinks button

Insert Access Data into a Word Document

1. In the Database window, click the table or query that you want to insert in a Word document.

2. Click the OfficeLinks drop-down arrow on the Database toolbar.

3. Click Merge It With MS Word.

4. Click the linking option button you want to use.

5. Click OK. If you selected the option for linking to an existing Word document, select the document.

6. In Word, click the Insert Merge Field button on the Mail Merge toolbar, and then click the field you want to insert. Repeat this step to insert as many fields as you need.

7. Click the Mail Merge Helper button on the Mail Merge toolbar, click the Merge button to display the Merge dialog box, and then click the Merge button.

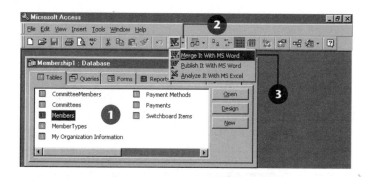

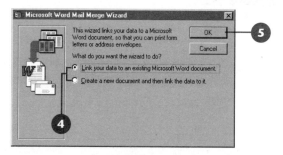

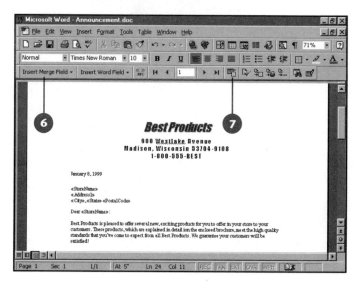

Create a Word Document from an Access Database

1. In the Database window, click the table, query, report, or form that you want to save as a Word document.

2. Click the OfficeLinks drop-down arrow on the Database toolbar.

3. Click Publish It With MS Word to save the data as a Rich Text Format file. Word opens and displays the document.

4. Edit the document using Word commands and features.

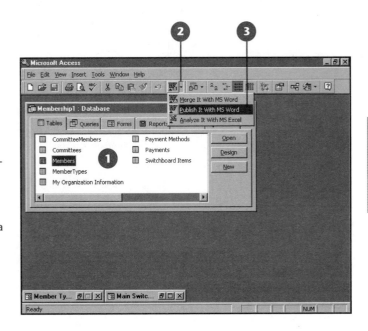

Analyzing Data in Excel

Before you can analyze Access data in a workbook, you must export the Access data to an Excel file. Exporting converts a copy of your open file into the file type of another program. In Excel, you can analyze the data using Excel's standard features and commands.

Format Access data in Excel. *When you use the Analyze It With MS Excel command, the output is saved as an Excel table in the folder in which Excel is stored on your system. Most of the formatting, such as fonts and colors, are retained in the Excel file.*

Insert an Access Table into Excel

1 In the Database window, click the table, query, report, or form that you want to analyze in Excel.

2 Click the OfficeLinks drop-down arrow on the Database toolbar.

3 Click Analyze It With MS Excel to save the table as an Excel file. Excel opens and displays the workbook.

4 Use Excel commands and features to edit and analyze the data.

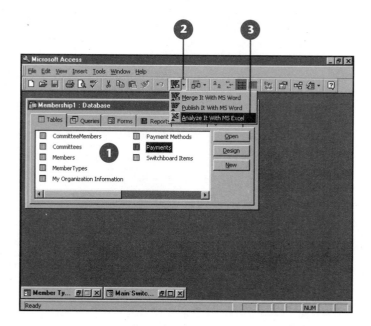

Creating Reports

To print a simple list of the records in your table, you can click the Print button. But if you want to include calculations, graphics, or a customized header or footer, you can create a report. A *report* is a summary of information in one or more Microsoft Access 97 tables. In many cases a report answers important questions about the contents of your database. For example, a report might tell you how many movies of each type have been rented each month or the amount of catalog sales made to your customers in Canada in the last quarter. In addition to providing detailed and summary information that can include calculations, reports also provide these features:

◆ Attractive formatting to help make your report easier to read and understand

◆ Charting and graphing to help illustrate the meaning of data

◆ Headers and footers that print identifying information at the top and bottom of every page

◆ Graphics to enhance the appearance of a report with clipart, photos, or scanned images

Exploring Different Ways to Create Reports

As with most objects you create in a database, you have several ways to create a report. With the AutoReport Wizards, Access creates a simple report (either columnar or tabular) based on the data in the currently selected table or query. With the Report Wizard you can specify the kind of report you want to create, and the Report Wizard guides you through each step of the process. All you do is answer a series of questions about your report, and Access builds a report with your data, using your formatting preferences.

Once you have completed a report, you can further customize it in Design view. As always, you can begin creating your report in Design view without using a wizard at all.

Click to create a report from scratch in Design view.

Click to create a report with the aid of the wizard.

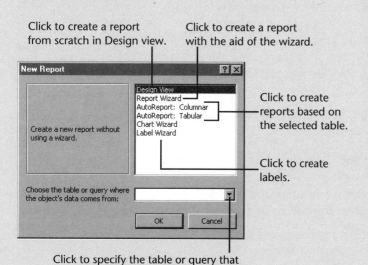

Click to create reports based on the selected table.

Click to create labels.

Create a new report without using a wizard.

Click to specify the table or query that contains the data you want to report.

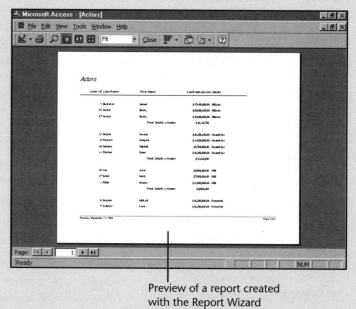

Preview of a report created with the Report Wizard

Modifying a Report in Design View

Sorting And Grouping button
Click to specify ways to group and sort records, and to hide or display grouping headers and footers.

AutoFormat button
Click to choose from a variety of formatting and layout options.

Formatting toolbar

Report header
This text appears at the top of the first page of the report.

Page header
This text appears at the top of each page of the report.

Grouping header
Any text here appears before each grouping of records.

Detail section
Fields to display for each detail record.

Design view Toolbox

Click to create new controls.

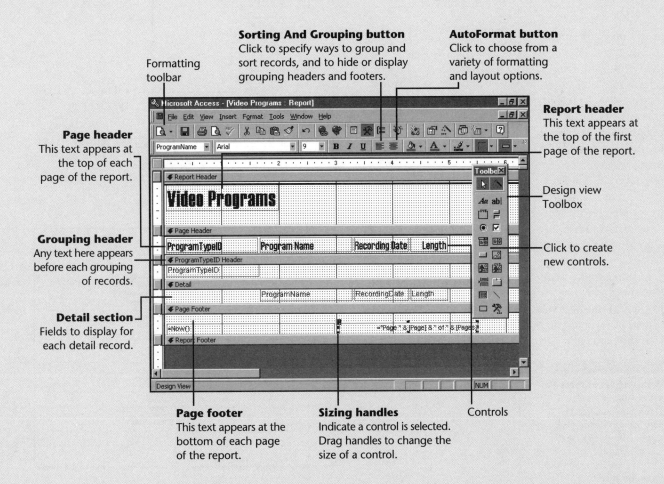

Page footer
This text appears at the bottom of each page of the report.

Sizing handles
Indicate a control is selected. Drag handles to change the size of a control.

Controls

Creating a Report the Easy Way

To create a simple report in Access, you can use the AutoReport Wizard. This wizard quickly arranges the data in the selected table or query as an attractively formatted report. In a report created with the AutoReport: Columnar wizard, each record's data is displayed vertically—that is, each field of data for each record appears on a line by itself. With the AutoReport: Tabular wizard, the data for each record is arranged horizontally with each field appearing in a column, as in Datasheet view. After creating a report, you can save and name it.

TIP

View the report in Print Preview. *When you create a report using the AutoReport Wizard, the report immediately appears in Print Preview, so that you can see what the report will look like when you print it. Click the Close button on the Print Preview toolbar to return to the Database window.*

Create a Report with the AutoReport Wizard

1 In the Database window, click the Reports tab, and then click New.

2 Click AutoReport: Columnar (to display records in a column) or click AutoReport: Tabular (to display records in rows).

3 Click the drop-down arrow for choosing a table or query on which to base the report, and then click the table or query you want.

4 Click OK.

After a moment, Access creates a report and displays it in the Print Preview window.

From Print Preview, you can save, print, or close the report, or you can switch to Design view to modify it.

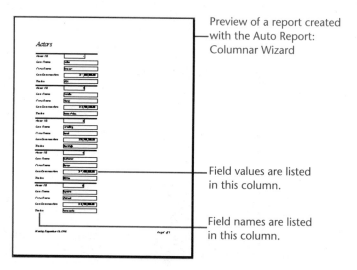

Preview of a report created with the Auto Report: Columnar Wizard

Field values are listed in this column.

Field names are listed in this column.

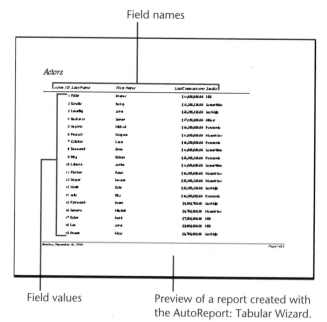

Field names

Field values

Preview of a report created with the AutoReport: Tabular Wizard.

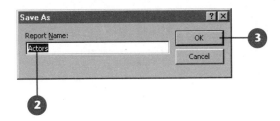

Preview multiple pages. *If your report contains more than one page, click the Multiple Pages button on the Print Preview toolbar, and then move the mouse to select the number and arrangement of pages you want to see.*

You don't have to save each report. *If you create a simple report with an AutoReport Wizard, and you make no further modifications to the report, consider not saving it in order to save space on your disk. You can easily re-create the report at any time.*

Create an instant report with the AutoReport command. *In the Database window, select the table or query that contains the data you want formatted as a report. Click the New Object drop-down arrow on the Database toolbar, and then click AutoReport. After a moment, Access generates a simple (but unformatted) columnar report.*

Save a Report

1 Click the Save button on the toolbar.

2 Type a name for your report.

3 Click OK.

9

Creating a Report Using the Report Wizard

The Report Wizard allows you to select the information you want presented in your report and choose from a variety of formatting options to determine how the report will look. Unlike the AutoReport Wizards, the Report Wizard lets you choose the specific fields (including fields from multiple tables or queries) you want to see in the report. Wizards remember your previous layout and formatting selections, so once you have established a style you like you will be able to move quickly through the wizard dialog boxes, accepting the default selections as you go.

Create a Report with the Report Wizard

1 On the Reports tab in the Database window, click New, and then click Report Wizard. You can also start the Report Wizard by clicking the Report option on the New Object drop-down list, and then clicking Report Wizard.

2 Click the Table/Queries drop-down arrow, and then click the table or query you want.

3 In the first Report Wizard dialog box, specify the fields that you want included in the report. You can include fields from other tables or queries by simply indicating the source of the fields.

4 Click Next to continue.

5 Specify how you want similar records grouped. You can choose any or all of the selected fields (up to ten fields) for grouping.

6 Click Next to continue.

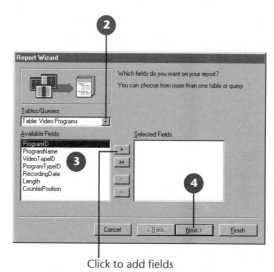

Click to add fields

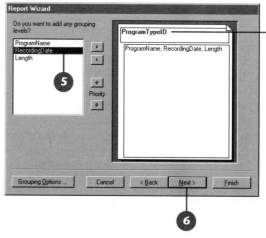

Field for primary grouping

TIP

Change the style of a report automatically. *After creating a report, change its style by using the AutoFormat command. Display your report in Design view, click the Format menu, click AutoFormat, choose one of the available styles for a report, and then click OK.*

TRY THIS

Create labels for names and addresses in your table. *In the New Report dialog box, choose Label Wizard and enter your preferences in the series of dialog boxes.*

6 Specify the order in which the records appear within each group. You can sort by up to four fields at a time, and specify ascending or descending order. Click Next to continue.

7 Indicate if you want to see summary information. If you choose to include summary calculations, you can choose from averages, counts, and minimum and maximum values. Click Next to continue.

8 Determine the arrangement and position of the information on the page, such as the page orientation. Click Next to continue.

9 Specify the style of the report, which affects its formatting and final appearance. Click Next to continue.

10 In the final wizard dialog box, you name your report and indicate whether you want to preview the report or display it in Design view.

11 Click Finish.

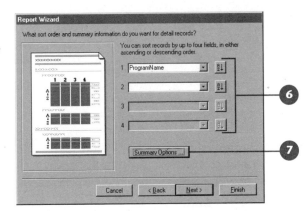

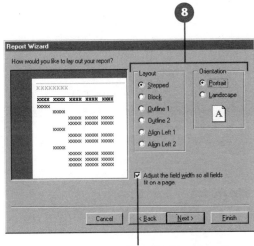

Clear this check box if you want to allow fields to flow to additional pages.

9

Working with Report Controls

Each item in a report—such as a field name, a field value, and the report title—is called a *control*. When you create a report with a wizard, the wizard arranges and sizes the controls to make a report according to the selections you provided. If you want to modify a report, you can do so in Design view by:

◆ Creating new controls

◆ Deleting controls

◆ Moving controls

◆ Sizing controls

◆ Changing control properties

◆ Changing the appearance of controls by formatting them, including applying borders and text effects such as bold and italics

◆ Adding borders and shading

Types of Report Controls

There are three kinds of controls you can use in a report:

◆ *Bound controls* are fields of data from the table or query. You cannot create a calculation in a bound control.

◆ *Unbound controls* are controls that contain a label or a text box. You can create calculations in an unbound control.

◆ *Calculated controls* are any values calculated in the report, including totals, subtotals, averages, percentages, and so on.

To create a control, you click the control button on the Toolbox for the kind of control you want to create, and then drag the pointer over the area where you want the control to appear. To delete a control, you click to select the control, and then press the Delete key.

Each type of control has specific characteristics you can change using the Properties feature. You simply select the control you want to modify, and then click the Properties button on the Report Design toolbar. In the Properties dialog box, you can specify the characteristics you want to change. Although there are menu commands and buttons you can use to change a specific characteristic, using the Properties button is a fast way to see all of the characteristics for a control and make several changes at once.

Label button
Click to create a label control.

Design view
tool box

Text Box button
Click to create an
unbound control and
a corresponding label.

Report displayed
in Design view

Drag this control pointer
to insert a new control.

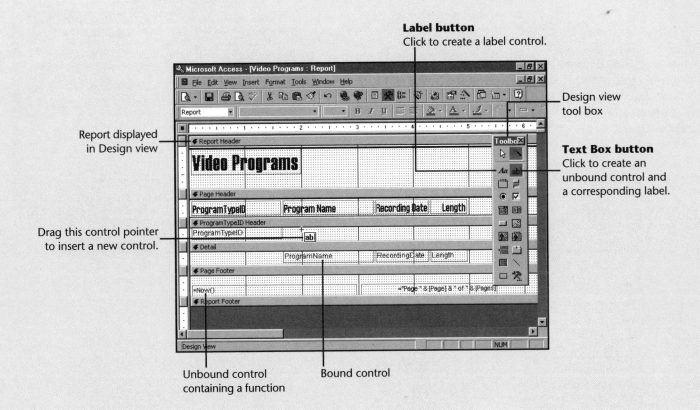

Unbound control
containing a function

Bound control

Changing the Spacing in a Report

You can improve the appearance of a report and make it easier to read by moving or sizing the controls to adjust the space between columns. For example, if your report contains one too many columns to fit on a single page, you might be able to reduce the size of some of the columns or the space between them so that all the columns fit on one page. Or if the report looks too cramped, you can increase the space between the columns by moving the controls further apart. You can even rearrange the columns by dragging the controls to a new location. In addition, you can adjust the amount of space between rows by moving the header bars.

Change the Spacing Between Columns of a Report

1. In the Design view in the detail section, click the control for the column name to display the control's sizing handles.

2. When the pointer shape changes to a hand, drag the column name in the appropriate direction to change the spacing.

3. In the page header section, click the control for the column name to display the control's sizing handles, and then repeat step 2.

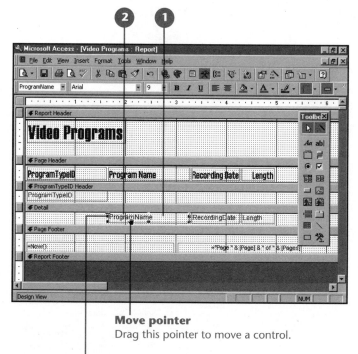

Move pointer
Drag this pointer to move a control.

Sizing handles
Indicate control is selected

Change the type of font.
Select a control, click the Font drop-down arrow on the Formatting toolbar, and then click the font name you want. For added emphasis, select a control and click the Bold, Italic, or Underline button on the Formatting toolbar. You can format a control with any one or all of these options. To remove this formatting from a control, select the control and click the button that corresponds to the formatting you want to remove.

Change the position of a control within a column.
Select the control and click the Align Left or Center button on the Formatting toolbar. If the control is in a header or footer, the control is aligned within the page margins.

Keep column headings aligned with controls in the detail section. *When you adjust the column width and the space between columns in the detail section of the report, be sure to also make the same adjustments in the page header section, so that the column headings appear directly over the data in the columns.*

Change Column Width

1 In the Design view in the detail section, click the control for the column name to display the control's sizing handles.

2 When the pointer shape changes to a two-headed arrow, drag in the appropriate direction to change the spacing.

3 In the page header section, click the control for the column name to display the control's sizing handles.

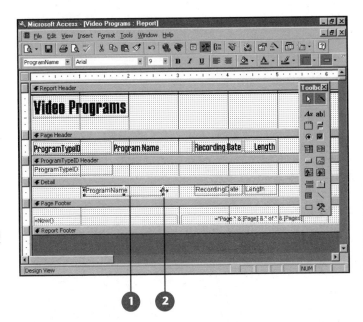

Changing the Spacing Between Parts of a Report

1 In Design view, position the pointer above the text where you want to change the spacing.

2 When the pointer shape changes to a two-headed arrow, drag in the appropriate direction to change the spacing.

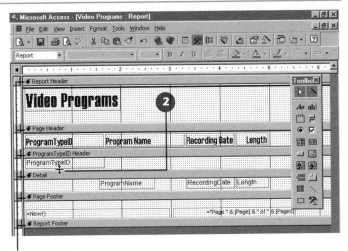

Drag to adjust the spacing between the parts of the report.

Creating Calculations in a Report

In addition to the built-in functions you can choose with the Report Wizard, you can use the *Expression Builder* to create your own calculations. By clicking buttons for the arithmetic operators you want to use and including constant values as needed, you can use the Expression Builder to further customize your report. For example, if you want to determine bonuses based on a percentage of sales, you can create an arithmetic expression to compute the results. When you generate the report, Access will perform the required calculations and display the results in the report. To display the calculations in the appropriate format, you can also use the Properties feature to specify formats for dates, currency, and other numeric data.

Choose Fields to Use in a Calculation

1. Display the report in Design view.

2. Create a Text Box control and position it where you want the calculated field to appear, or select an existing unbound control.

3. Click the Properties button on the Report Design toolbar.

4. Click in the Control Source field, and then click the Expression Builder button.

5. Click the equal sign (=) button.

6. Click the button corresponding to the calculation you want or click the Operators folder, click the Arithmetic folder, and then click the operator you want to use.

7. Double-click the field (or fields) you want to use in the calculation, or click the folder containing the fields you want to use and choose those fields.

8. Type any other values (constants) you want to include in the expression.

9. Click OK to insert the calculation in the field.

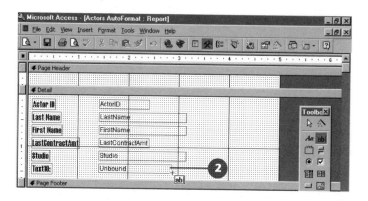

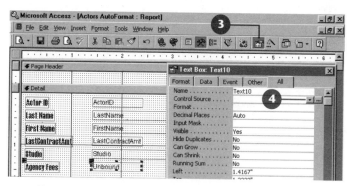

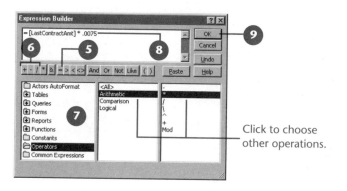

Click to choose other operations.

Format Values in a Report

1 In Design view, position the insertion point in the field whose format you want to change, and then click the Properties button on the Report Design toolbar.

2 On either the All tab or the Format tab of the Properties dialog box, click the right side of the Format box, and then select the format you want to use.

The names of the formats appear on the left side of the drop-down list and examples of the corresponding formats appear on the right side.

3 If you are formatting a number (rather than a date), in the Decimal Places box, enter the number of decimal places you want.

4 Click the Close button.

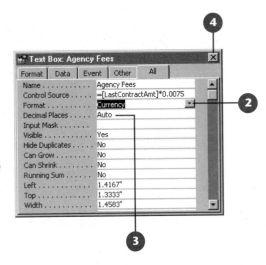

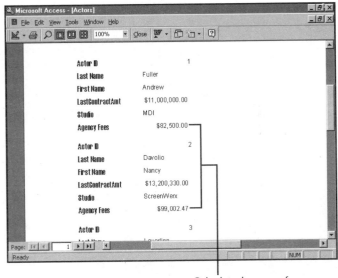

Calculated agency fees

9

Grouping Records in a Report

When you create a report with the Report Wizard, you can choose to group like records together to obtain subtotals and other calculations for each group. For example, in a report of sales representative sales figures for a year, you might group the representatives' sales by month. In this way, you can easily determine who was the top achiever each month. In another report, you could group all the sales representatives' results together to see trends for the representatives' performance over a whole year. Even if you create your report from scratch or decide to group records later, you can use the Sorting And Grouping feature to further organize information in your report.

Group Records

1 Display the report in Design view.

2 Click the Sorting And Grouping button on the Report Design toolbar.

3 Click the right side of the Field/Expression column, and then choose a field for grouping records.

4 Click the right side of the Sort Order column, and then choose either ascending or descending order for sorting the groups of records.

5 Click the right side of the Group Header field, and then choose Yes if you want to include a header that will separate the start of each group of records.

6 Click the right side of the Group Footer field, and then choose Yes if you want to include a footer that will separate the end of each group of records. Choose this option if you want to include a subtotal or summary calculation for each group of records.

7 Click the Close button.

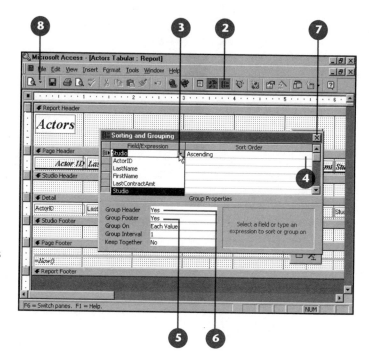

8 Click the Preview button on the Report Design toolbar.

9 Click the Zoom button to change magnification.

10 Click the Close button on the Preview toolbar to return to Design view.

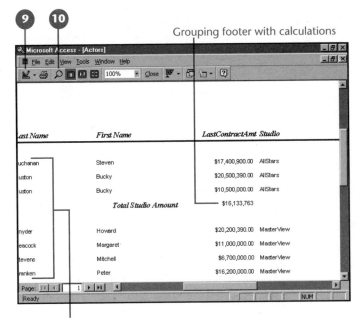

Grouping footer with calculations

Grouped records in a report

Previewing a Report

To get the complete picture of what a report will look like when you print it, you can display the report in Print Preview by clicking the Print Preview button (when you are in Design view). After completing the Report Wizard, you have the option of displaying the report in Print Preview. And after you create a report using AutoReport, the view changes to Print Preview, already in the magnified view, in which you see a close-up view of the report.

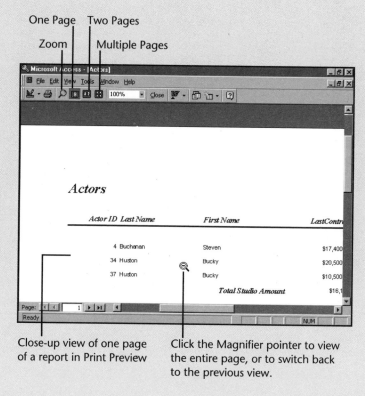

One Page Two Pages

Zoom Multiple Pages

Close-up view of one page of a report in Print Preview

Click the Magnifier pointer to view the entire page, or to switch back to the previous view.

CHANGING THE MAGNIFICATION IN PRINT PREVIEW	
To:	**Do this:**
Increase the magnification Preview	Click the Zoom button on the Print Preview toolbar.
Return to the previous magnification	Click the Zoom button on the Print Preview toolbar.
Display the entire page in the Print Preview window	Click the One Page button on the Print Preview toolbar.
Display two pages side-by-side	Click the Two Pages button on the Print Preview toolbar.
Display multiple pages of a report	Click the Multiple Pages button on the Print Preview toolbar, and drag the mouse to select the number and arrangement of pages you want to see.

Click the Magnifier
pointer to get a close-up
view of the page.

Single page of a report
in Print Preview

Click to display two pages side-by-side

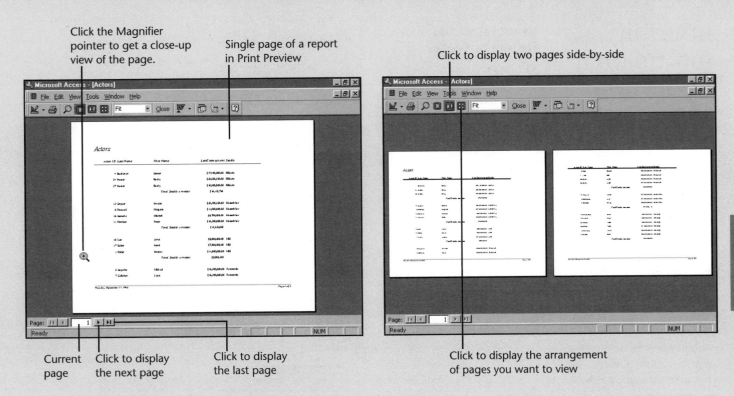

Current
page

Click to display
the next page

Click to display
the last page

Click to display the arrangement
of pages you want to view

Inserting Information in Headers and Footers

Headers in a report display text at the top of each page or at the top of the report. *Footers* appear at the bottom of the page. Headers and footers can also appear at the start and end of records you have grouped together. As with other controls in a report, you can change the formatting of the text and controls in headers and footers. You can also add new controls (called fields) that insert specific kinds of information automatically when you generate a report. In addition, you can use commands on the Insert menu to insert page numbers and data and time information.

Build button

Insert Information in a Header or Footer

1 In Design view, click the Text Box button on the Toolbox, and then drag a text box control to the area in the header or footer where you want the information to appear.

2 With the control still selected, click the Build button on the Report Design toolbar, and then click Expression Builder.

3 Double-click the Common Expressions folder.

4 Double-click the expression you want to insert.

5 Click OK to insert your expression.

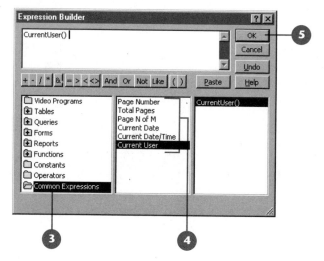

Printing a Report

Printing a report is as simple as clicking a button. Clicking the Print button toolbar prints one copy of all pages of the report. If you want to print only selected pages or if you want to specify other printing options, use the Print command on the File menu.

SEE ALSO

See "Previewing a Report" on page 124 for information about previewing a report before printing.

Print a Report

1 Click the File menu, and then click Print.

2 If necessary, click the Printer Name drop-down arrow, and then select the printer you want to use.

3 To print all the pages in a report, make sure the All option button is selected; or to specify certain pages in the report to print, click the Pages option button, and then type the page numbers in the From and To text boxes.

4 If you want more than one copy to print, click the Number Of Copies spin arrows to indicate the number of copies.

5 Click OK.

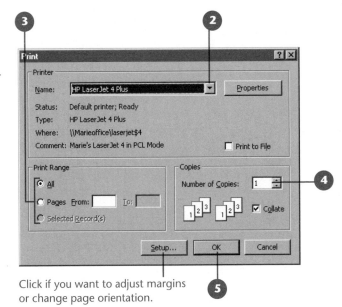

Click if you want to adjust margins or change page orientation.

Creating Forms

Forms provide another way for you to enter and maintain data in a table. Instead of entering records in the grid of rows and columns in Datasheet view, you can use a form that can represent a paper form. Such a form can minimize data entry errors because it closely resembles the paper-based form containing the information you want to enter in your table. In addition, if your table contains fields that include graphics, documents, or objects from other programs, you can see the actual objects in Form view. (In Datasheet view, the object is identified with text or with an icon.) To make it even easier to enter and maintain data, you can also include instructions and guidance on the form so that a user of the form knows how to complete it. You can add borders and graphics to the form, as well, to enhance its appearance.

Creating Access Forms

When you create a database using a wizard, you can select a style for the forms that the wizard creates for you. Similarly, when you create a table with the Table Wizard, the wizard automatically creates a form that you can use to enter data into a table. However, in addition to using the forms that Access automatically creates as part of a wizard, you can also create forms yourself.

As with most objects you create in a database, you have several ways to create a form. You can use the *AutoForm* command to quickly create a simple form that contains all the fields in the currently selected table or query. With the *AutoForm Wizards,* Access creates a simple form (columnar, tabular, or datasheet) based on the table or query you specify. With the *Form Wizard,* you can specify the kind of form you want to create and the wizard guides you through each step of the process. All you do is answer a series of questions about your form, and Access creates a form using your formatting preferences. Of course, once you have completed a form, you can further customize it in Design view. As always, you can begin creating your form in Design view without using the wizard at all.

Click to create a form from scratch in Design view.

Click to create a form with the aid of the wizard.

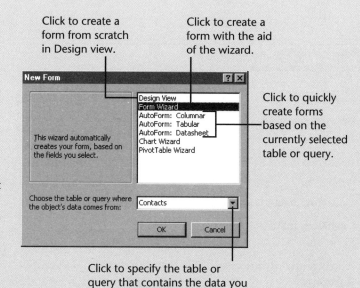

Click to quickly create forms based on the currently selected table or query.

Click to specify the table or query that contains the data you want displayed in a form.

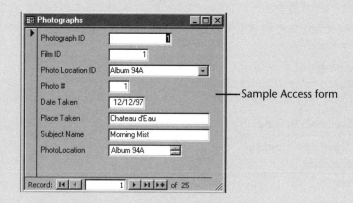

Sample Access form

Working with Form Controls

Each item on a form, such as a field name, a field value, and the form title, is called a *control*. When you create a form with a wizard, the wizard takes care of arranging and sizing the controls to make a form according to the selections you provided to the wizard. If you want to modify a form, you can do so in Design view by:

◆ Moving and sizing controls

◆ Changing control properties

◆ Changing the appearance of controls with borders, shading, and text effects such as bold and italics

◆ Inserting new controls

◆ Organizing controls using group boxes

Types of Form Controls

There are three kinds of controls you can use in a form:

◆ *Bound controls* are fields of data from a table or query. A form must contain a bound control for each field that you want to appear on the form. You cannot create a calculation in a bound control.

◆ *Unbound controls* are controls that contain a label or a text box. Typically, you use unbound controls to identify other controls or areas on the form. You can create calculations from an unbound control.

◆ *Calculated controls* are any values calculated in the form, including totals, subtotals, averages, percentages, and so on.

To create a control, you click the control button for the kind of control you want to create and then drag the pointer over the area where you want the control to appear. The control buttons are available on the Toolbox in Design view.

In Design view, you see two parts for every control: the control itself and its corresponding label. When you drag a control to position it, its corresponding label moves with it (and vice versa). You cannot separate a label from its control.

If you are unsure of how to create controls, you can click the Control Wizard button on the Toolbox to activate the Control Wizards. With the Control Wizards active, a wizard guides you through the process of creating certain types of controls. For example, if you create a list box control with the Control Wizards button active, the wizard appears, providing information about this type of control. It also prompts you to enter a name for the control label. To turn off the Control Wizards, click the Control Wizards button again (so that it is no longer indented).

Each different type of form control has specific characteristics you can change using the Properties feature. You simply select the control you want to modify and then click the Properties button on the Form Design toolbar. In the Properties dialog box, you can specify the characteristics you want to change.

10

Creating a Form the Easy Way

To create a simple form in Access, you can use one of the AutoForm Wizards. These wizards quickly arrange the fields from the selected table or query as an attractively formatted form. In a form created with the AutoForm: Columnar wizard, you see each record's data displayed vertically—that is, each field of data for each record appears on a line by itself. With the AutoForm: Tabular wizard, you see each record's data horizontally, with each field appearing in a column. With the AutoForm: Datasheet wizard the form displays the records in Datasheet view. After you create a form, you can save and name it so that you can use it again. Any form you save is listed on the Forms tab of the Database window.

Create a Simple Form with the AutoForm Wizard

1 In the Database window, click the Forms tab, and then click New.

2 Click AutoForm: Columnar (to display records in a column), or click AutoForm: Tabular (to display records in rows), or click AutoForm: Datasheet (to display records in Datasheet view).

3 Click the drop-down arrow for choosing a table or query on which to base the form, and then click the name of the table or query you want.

4 Click OK.

After a moment, Access creates a form and displays it in Form view.

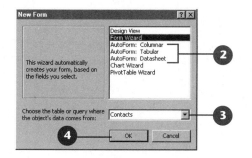

Form created with the AutoForm: Columnar Wizard

Field names

Field values

Form created with the AutoForm: Tabular Wizard

Field values

Field names

Create a form instantly with the AutoForm command. *In the Database window, open the table or query that contains the data you want to display in a form. Click the New Object drop-down arrow on the Database toolbar, and then click AutoForm. After a moment, Access generates a simple (but unformatted) columnar form.*

PhotographID	FilmID	PhotoLocationID	Pho	DateTak	PlaceTaken
1	1	Album 94A	1	12/12/97	Chateau d'Eau
2	1	Album 94A	2	12/12/97	Notre Dame
3	1	Album 94A	3	12/15/97	Louvre
4	1	Album 94A	4	12/15/97	Arch of Stars
5	1	Album 94A	5	12/15/97	Eiffel Tower
6	2	Album 90A	1	2/3/98	Mt. McKinley
7	2	Album 90A	2	3/3/98	Peak Lake
8	2	Album 90A	3	12/2/98	Sunrise Ridge
9	2	Album 90A	4	4/1/98	Eskimo Hill
10	2	Album 90A	5	9/9/98	Ridgeville Valley
11	3	Album 95	1	2/2/96	Cane Patchy
12	3	Album 95	2	4/20/96	Little Village
13	3	Album 95	3	4/22/96	Island Greenville
14	3	Album 95	4	4/26/96	Palm Grove
15	3	Album 95	5	4/26/96	Cane Farm
16	4	Album 95	1	11/11/97	Cologne, Germany
17	4	Album 95	2	11/11/97	Berlin, Germany

Record: 1 of 25

Save a Form

1 With the form displayed, click the Save button on the Form View toolbar.

2 In the Save As dialog box, type the name for your form.

3 Click OK.

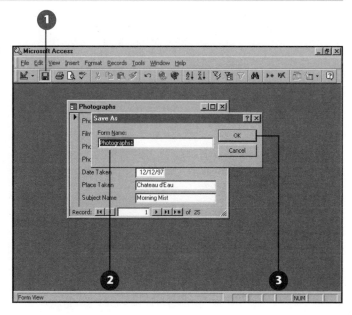

Creating a Custom Form

The *Form Wizard* lets you select the information you want to include in your form and choose from a variety of formatting options to determine how you want the form to look. You can choose the specific fields (including fields from multiple tables or queries) you want to see in the form. When you enter information in a form, the new data will be stored in the correct tables.

TIP

Include most of the fields quickly. *To include all but a few fields, click the Move All button (>>). Then, on the right side of the dialog box, click the field you want to exclude, and then click the Remove button (<). Do this for each field you want to exclude. Of course, to exclude all the fields, you can click the Remove All button (<<).*

1. On the Forms tab in the Database window, click New, and then double-click Form Wizard.

2. Click the drop-down arrow for choosing a table or query on which to base the form, and then click the name of the table or query you want.

3. In the first Form Wizard dialog box, specify the fields that you want included in the form by double-clicking the fields.

4. Click Next to continue.

5. Determine the arrangement and position of the information on the form (columnar, tabular, datasheet, justified). In the preview area of the dialog box, you can see a preview of your layout choice. Click Next to continue.

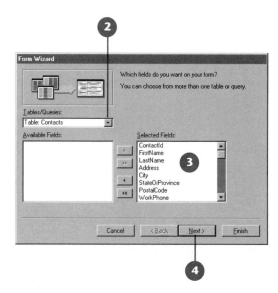

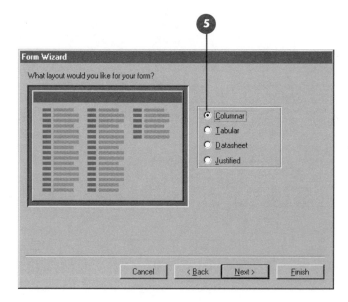

The Form Wizard remembers previous selections.

The Form Wizard remembers your previous layout and style preferences. Once you have established a style you like, then you will be able to move quickly through the wizard dialog boxes, accepting the default selections as you go.

6 Specify the style of the form, which affects its formatting and final appearance. In the preview area of the dialog box, you can see a preview of the selected style. Click Next to continue.

7 In the final wizard dialog box, enter a name for your form.

8 Indicate whether you want to open the form or display it in Design view.

9 Click Finish.

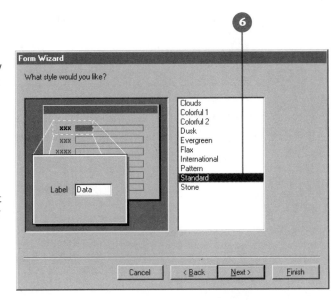

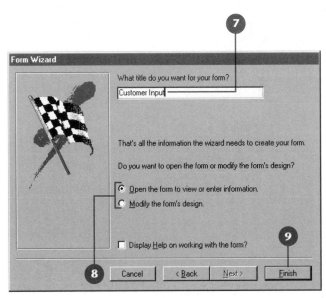

Creating a Form from Scratch

Although a wizard can be a big help when you are first learning to create a form, you do not need to use the wizard. If you prefer, you can create a form without the help of a wizard. Instead of answering questions in a series of dialog boxes, you can start working in Design View right away. You can create and modify controls, and move and format the controls, to create the exact form you want.

SEE ALSO

See "Adding and Removing Controls" on page 137 to learn how to insert new controls on a form and delete existing controls.

Create a Form from Scratch

1. In the Database window, click the Forms tab, and then click New.

2. In the New Form dialog box, click Design View, and then choose the table or query from where the data will come. Click OK.

3. Click the Field List button on the Form Design toolbar to add a bound control for the field you want to display in the form.

4. Select the field you want to add to the form.

5. Drag the field to the location in the form where you want the field to appear, and then release the mouse button to position the field.

6. Create new controls as needed.

7. Format the text in the form, as needed.

8. Click the Save button on the Form Design toolbar to name the form and save it in the database.

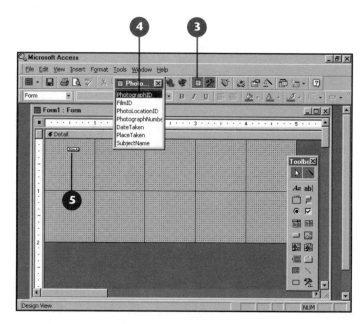

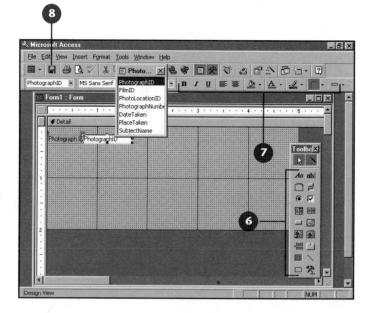

Adding and Removing Controls

You can make a form easier to use by adding controls to it. Controls also can improve the appearance of a form and display additional information on a form. To create a control on a form, you click the appropriate control button on the Toolbox. The Toolbox appears by default in Design view. However, if the Toolbox was closed for some reason, you need to redisplay it when you want to create new controls on a form. With the control pointer, drag in the form where you want the control to appear. You can also delete controls that you no longer want on the form.

SEE ALSO

See "Modifying a Form in Design View" on page 139 for more information on using this feature.

Add Controls to a Form

1. In Design view, display the Toolbox.

2. Click the button on the Toolbox for the type of control you want to create.

3. In the Form window, click and drag the pointer to draw a box in the location where you want the control to appear, and then release the mouse button.

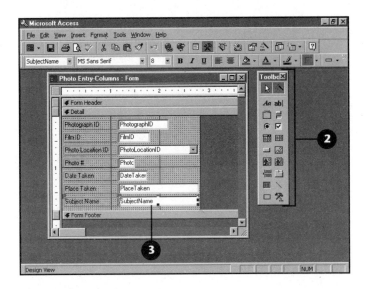

Remove Controls from a Form

1. In Design view, display the Toolbox.

2. Click the control you want to delete to select it. Small black boxes, called *handles,* appear around the control to indicate it is selected.

3. Press Delete.

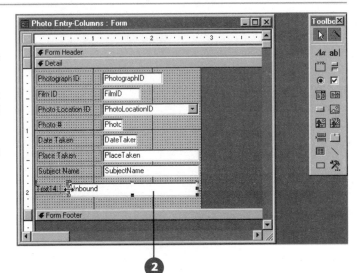

Displaying a Form in Design View

After you create a form, you might decide to modify certain features (called controls) in the form to make it easier to use. For example, you might want more descriptive labels to identify each field. Or you might create a box around a group of fields to help the user identify and complete related fields. To modify a form, you must display the form in Design view, which you can do from the Forms tab in the Database window or from Form view. The View button lets you switch between Form view and Design view so that you can easily modify a form and view the results.

> **SEE ALSO**
>
> *See "Using Toolbox Buttons and Controls" on page 140 for more information on controls.*

Display a Form in Design View

1 In the Database window, click the Forms tab.

2 Click the form you want to use.

3 Click Design.

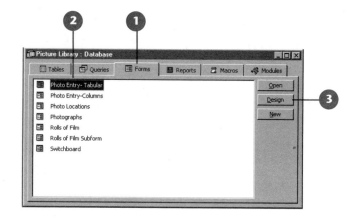

Switch Between Views

1 In Design view, click the View button to display the form in Form view so you can enter information.

2 In Form view, click the View button to display the form in Design view so you can modify the form.

View button
Click to switch between views.

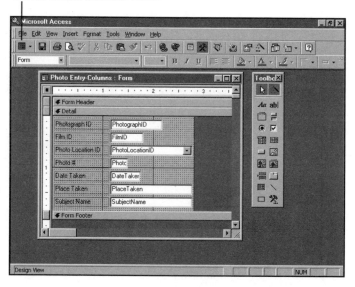

Modifying a Form in Design View

Field List button
Click to add new fields to the form.

Toolbox button
Click to display or hide the Toolbox.

AutoFormat button
Click to choose from a variety of formatting and layout options.

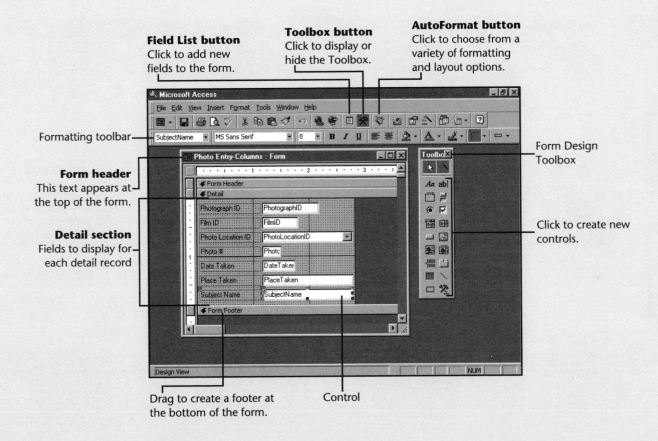

Formatting toolbar

Form Design Toolbox

Form header
This text appears at the top of the form.

Click to create new controls.

Detail section
Fields to display for each detail record

Drag to create a footer at the bottom of the form.

Control

Using Toolbox Buttons and Controls

Button	Button Name	Description
	Select Objects	Click this button, and then click the control you want to select. To select multiple controls that are grouped together, click this button, and then drag a rectangle shape around all the controls you want to select.
	Control Wizards	Click to use control wizards when they are available.
	Text Box	This button creates a text box in which the user can enter text (or numbers) for this field in the record. Use this control for fields assigned a text or number data type.
	Label	This button creates a text label. Because the other controls already include a corresponding label, use this button to create labels that are independent of other controls, such as text needed for user instructions or the name of the form in a heading.
	Option Group	This button creates a box around a group of option buttons. The user is only allowed to make one selection from the buttons enclosed by a group box.
	Toggle Button	This button creates a button that allows the user to make a yes or no selection by pushing in the toggle button. Use this control for fields assigned the yes/no data type.
	Option Button	This button creates an option button (also known as a radio button) that allows the user to make a single selection from at least two choices. Use this control for fields assigned the yes/no data type.
	Check Box	This button creates a check box that allows a user to make multiple yes or no selections. Use this control for fields assigned the yes/no data type.
	List Box	This button creates a list box that allows a user to select from a list of options. You can enter your own options in the list or you can have another table provide a list of options.

TOOLBOX BUTTONS

Button	Button Name	Description
	Combo Box	This button creates a combo box in which the user has the option to enter text or select from a list of options. You can enter your own options in the list or you can display options stored in another table.
	Command Button	This button creates a button that runs a macro or Visual Basic function when the user pushes the button in the form.
	Image	This button inserts a frame in which you can insert a graphic in your form.Use this control when you want to insert a graphic that remains the same in all the records displayed in this form, such as clipart or a logo.
	Bound Object Frame	This button inserts an OLE object from another source within the same database. Use this button to insert an object that is linked to another source in the database and needs to be updated to reflect recent changes.
	Unbound Object Frame	This button inserts an OLE object from another source. Use this button to insert an object that is linked to another program and needs to be updated to reflect recent changes.
	Page Break	This button forces the fields that start at the insertion point to appear on the next screen.
	Tab Control	This button creates a tab in your form. Creating tabs in a form gives your form the appearance of a dialog box in a program so that related controls can appear together on their own tab.
	Line	This creates a line that you draw on the form.
	Subform/Subreport	This button inserts another form within the current form at the insertion point.
	Rectangle	This button creates a rectangle or border that you draw on the form.
	More Controls	Click to display other Toolboxes.

10

Sizing and Moving Controls in a Form

When you select a control on a form *sizing handles* appear on the sides and at the corners of the control. You can drag the sizing handles to adjust the size of the control. You can also drag inside a selected control to move the control to a new location.

TIP

Change the size in two directions at once. *You can change the height and width of a control at the same time by dragging a corner sizing handle.*

Change the Size of a Control

1. Display the form in Design view.

2. Click the control you want to resize.

3. Position the pointer over a sizing handle until the pointer shape changes to a two-headed arrow.

4. With the sizing pointer, drag to resize the control.

   For example, to make the control wider, drag the sizing handle on the center right of the control further to the right.

5. Release the mouse button.

Sizing handles
Indicate a control is selected

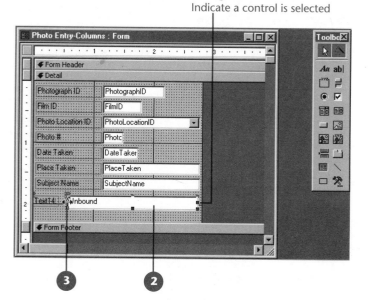

TIP

Select multiple controls. *To select controls that are next to each other, click the Select Objects button on the Toolbox, and then drag a rectangle around the controls you want to select. To select controls that are not next to each other, press the Shift key as you click each control.*

SEE ALSO

See "Displaying a Form Design View" on page 138 for more information about the Design View.

Move a Control

1 Display the form in Design view.

2 Click the control you want to move.

3 Position the pointer over an edge of a control until the pointer shape changes to a hand. This pointer is the move pointer.

4 With the move pointer, drag the control in the direction you want to go.

5 Release the mouse button when the control is located where you want.

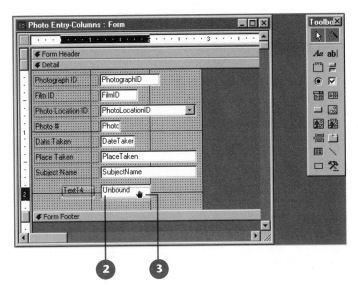

Using the Control Wizards

Although there are many controls you can create on a form, the procedures for creating each control are quite similar, with minor variations depending on the type of control. When you want to include a list of valid options for a field on a form, you can create either a *combo box* or *list box* control. Both controls provide a list from which a user can choose when entering data. The easiest way to create either of these controls is with the Control Wizards activated.

Create a List Box or Combo Box

1 Display the form in Design view. Make sure the Toolbox is displayed.

2 Click the Control Wizards button on the Toolbox, if this button is not already selected.

3 Click the Combo Box or List Box button on the Toolbox.

4 In the Form window, click and drag the mouse to create a rectangle in the location where you want the control to appear. When you release the mouse button, the wizard dialog box for the selected control appears.

5 Specify how you want the control to get its values.

6 Click Next to continue.

7 Select the table that contains the values you want displayed in the list or combo box, and then click Next to continue.

8 Select the field that contains the values you want displayed in the list or combo box, and then click Next to continue.

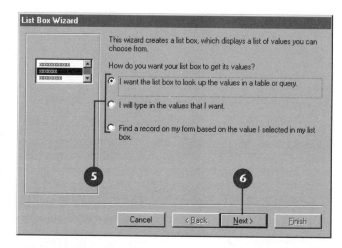

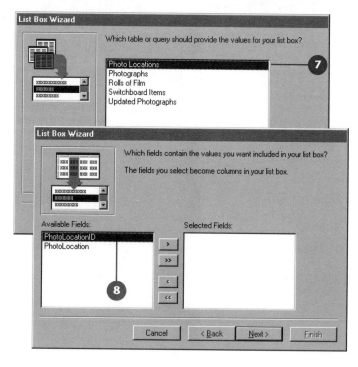

Specify values from a different table or query in the database. *If you have chosen the third option in step 5, you can specify values from a different table or query. Select the table or query from which you want the control to retrieve its values. Click Next to continue. Double-click the field (or fields) you want to include, and then click Next to continue.*

9 Specify the width of the columns for the list box, and then click Next to continue.

10 Specify whether or not you want Access to store the value that the user enters in a field, and then click Next to continue.

11 Enter a label for the new control, and then click Finish.

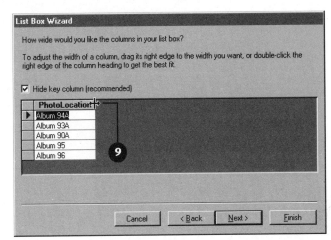

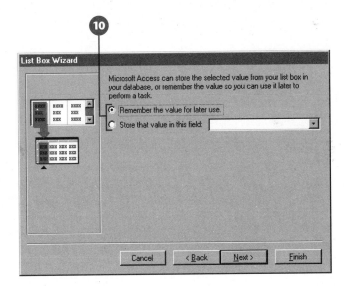

Improving the Appearance of Forms and Reports

The wizards you can use to create databases, reports, and forms provide attractive formatting to these objects. However, you might decide to further enhance a report or form by adding or modifying different formatting, layout, and style options. In addition, if you create forms or reports from scratch in Design view, you can enhance the basic controls by applying special effects and other formatting features to give your customized reports or forms the exact look you want. You can also add borders and shading to your reports and forms.

For information about adding graphics (from a clipart library, from another graphics files, or graphics you create yourself) to your reports and forms, see section 12, "Adding Graphics to Forms and Reports"

Identifying Ways to Enhance Forms and Reports

Click to display a form or report in Design view

New text color

Border created around text

Filled box

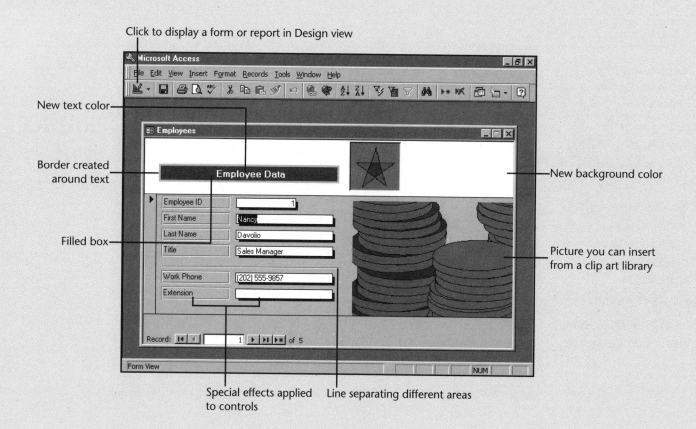

New background color

Picture you can insert from a clip art library

Special effects applied to controls

Line separating different areas

Click to change the font, font size, style attributes, or alignment.

Click to change the thickness of lines or borders.

Click to apply a special effect to buttons and other controls.

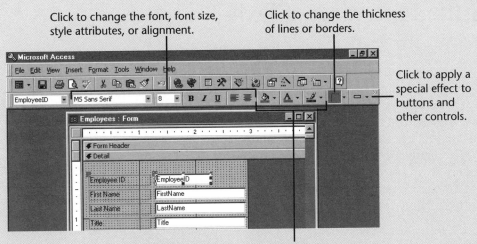

Click to change the color of background, text, or lines and borders.

If the Toolbox is not displayed on your screen, click the View menu, click Toolbars, and then click Toolbox.

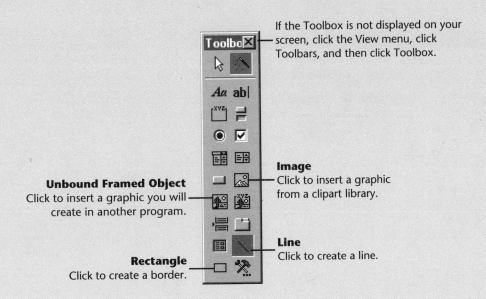

Unbound Framed Object
Click to insert a graphic you will create in another program.

Image
Click to insert a graphic from a clipart library.

Line
Click to create a line.

Rectangle
Click to create a border.

11

Changing the Appearance of Text

In Design view, you can change the appearance of the text in a report or form so that it makes a greater visual impact or is easier to read. For example, you can increase the size of the text or change its font type. You can also change the alignment, which is the position of the text within its control. Just select the control whose formatting you want to change, and then click the appropriate button on the Formatting toolbar.

Formatting toolbar

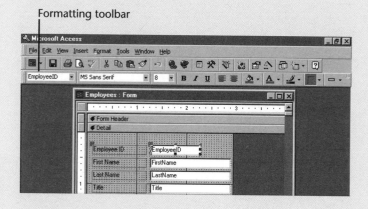

CHANGE THE APPEARANCE OF TEXT	
To change this:	**Select the text by clicking its control, and then do this:**
Font size	Click the Font Size drop-down arrow on the Formatting toolbar, and then click the size you want. The larger the number, the larger the size of the characters. You can also type a number in the Font Size box.
Font type	Click the Font drop-down arrow on the Formatting toolbar, and then click the font type you want.
Text alignment	Click the Align Left or Center button on the Formatting toolbar.
Emphasis	Click the Bold, Italic, or Underline button on the Formatting toolbar. You can format your text with any one or all of these options.

Formatting a Form or Report the Easy Way

A fast way to format a form or report is with the *AutoFormat* button. When you click this button on the Design toolbar, you can select and preview a variety of layouts and styles. After making your selections, Access formats the entire report or form consistently for you. After using AutoFormat, you can always make additional changes to the formatting.

AutoFormat Button

Format a Form with AutoFormat

1 Display the form you want to format in Design view.

2 Click the AutoFormat button on the Form Design toolbar.

3 In the AutoFormat dialog box, enter your formatting preferences for the form.

4 Click OK.

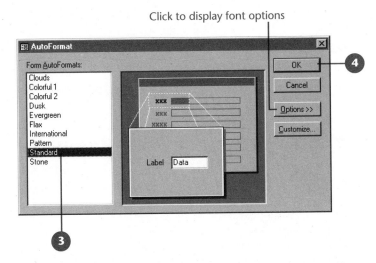

Click to display font options

Format a Report with AutoFormat

1 Display the report you want to format in Design view.

2 Click the AutoFormat button on the Report Design toolbar.

3 In the AutoFormat dialog box, enter your formatting preferences for the report.

4 Click OK.

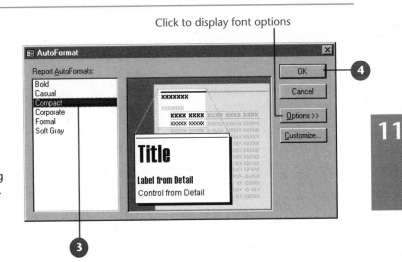

Click to display font options

Adding Lines and Borders

In a form or report that contains a lot of information, you can make the form or report easier to read by adding lines between sections or by adding borders around a group of controls. Lines and borders help your reader organize the information so that the report is easier to read or so the form is easier to fill out.

TIP

Draw multiple lines and borders. *To draw several lines or borders, double-click the Line button or the Rectangle button. The tool you selected remains in effect until you click the button again, or click another button.*

TIP

Adjust the length of a line or the size of a border. *Position the pointer over a sizing handle, and then drag in the direction in which you want to resize the line or border.*

Add a Line to a Form or Report

1. Display the form or report in Design view.

2. Click the Line button on the Toolbox.

3. With the Line pointer, drag a line where you want the line to appear, and then release the mouse button.

   Sizing handles appear at each end of the line.

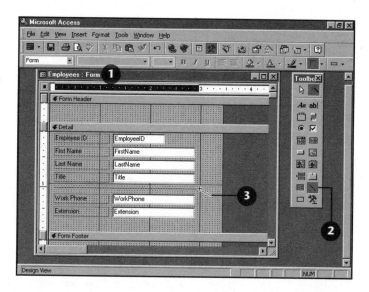

Add a Border to a Form or Report

1. Display the form or report in Design view.

2. Click the Rectangle button on the Toolbox.

3. With the Rectangle pointer, drag a rectangle where you want the border to appear, and then release the mouse button.

   Sizing handles appear at each corner and on each side of the border.

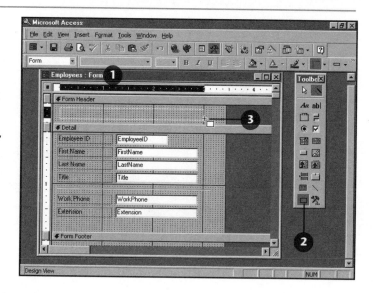

Changing the Thickness of Lines and Borders

After you create a line or border, you can adjust the thickness of the lines with the Line/Border Width button. After you make a choice on many of the Formatting toolbar buttons, such as Line/Border Width, any similar objects you create next will be formatted with the currently selected formatting, as indicated on the toolbar button.

TRY THIS

Select or create a line or border in a report or form. *Click the Line/Border Width drop-down arrow on the Formatting toolbar, and then select the smallest thickness to create a hairline thin line. Then select the largest border width. Notice the difference between the smallest and greatest border width.*

Change the Thickness of a Line or Border

1 Display the form or report in Design view.

2 Select the line or border whose line thickness you want to adjust.

3 Click the Line/Border Width drop-down arrow on the Formatting toolbar, and then select the thickness you want.

If you want to format an existing object with the currently selected formatting, you can simply select the object, and then click the appropriate button on the Formatting toolbar—you don't need to click the button's drop-down arrow and repeat your selection from the menu.

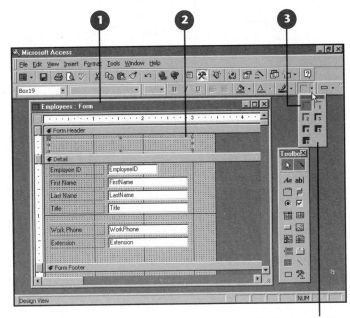

The greater number, the thicker the line.

11

Changing Colors

Choosing appropriate colors for your form or report is an important formatting decision. For example, the colors on a form should guide users in filling out the form on the screen. Also, if you have a color printer available, you can significantly enhance the appearance of a report or form by adding color to lines or text. You can also add color to fill in rectangles. In addition, you can add a background color to entire areas (such as a header, footer, or detail area) of the report or form.

TIP

Make borders around a colored rectangle disappear. *Select the colored rectangle, click the Line/Border Color button on the Formatting toolbar, and then click Transparent.*

Change the Color of a Line or Border

1 Display the form or report in Design view.

2 Select the line or border whose color you want to change.

3 Click the Line/Border Color drop-down arrow on the Formatting toolbar, and then select the color you want.

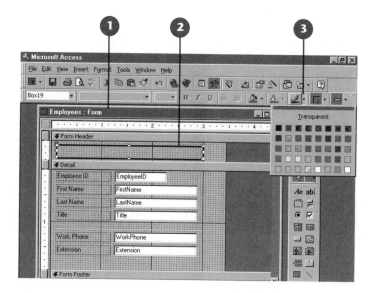

Add Color Inside a Border

1 Display the form or report in Design view.

2 Select the border in which you want to apply a color.

3 Click the Fill/Back Color drop-down arrow on the Formatting toolbar, and then select the color you want.

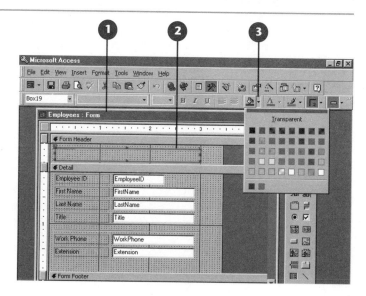

Rearrange layers of objects. *If filling a rectangle with color obscures the text, you can make the rectangle appear behind the text so that it doesn't block the text. Simply select the rectangle, click the Format menu, and then click Send To Back.*

Use color in a report or form. *Create a bright blue rectangle around some text in a report or form. Fill the rectangle with yellow. On the Format menu, click Send To Back.*

Align controls and lines the way you want. *When you first work in Design view, the controls and other objects you create align themselves along an invisible grid as you move them. To gain greater control over the exact placement of lines and controls, you can turn off the Snap To Grid option. Click the Format menu, and then click Snap To Grid to deactivate this feature. Click this command again to activate it.*

Add Color to Text

1 Display the form or report in Design view.

2 Select the text whose color you want to change.

3 Click the Font/Fore Color drop-down arrow on the Formatting toolbar, and then select the color you want. To ensure that the text remains visible in a colored rectangle, do not choose a color that is the same as the rectangle itself.

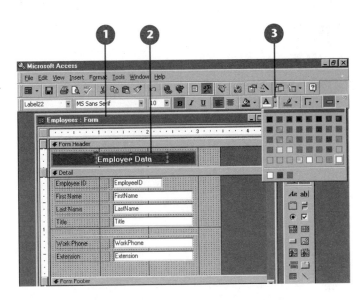

Change the Background Color

1 Display the form or report in Design view.

2 Click in the header, footer, or detail area whose color you want to change.

Be sure not to click an existing control or object so that you do not change its color instead of the background color.

3 Click the Fill/Back Color drop-down arrow on the Formatting toolbar, and then select the color you want.

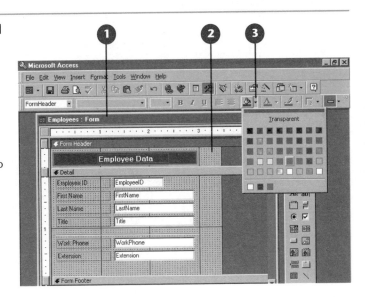

11

Applying Special Effects to Controls

You can apply special effects to one or more controls in a form or report to enhance the appearance of the form or report. For example, you can create three-dimensional effects, including flat (the default effect), raised, sunken, etched, shadowed, and chiseled. Use the effect that seems most appropriate for the tone of the form or report. For example, in a more formal financial report, you might choose the simple flat effect. In a report outlining future technology needs, consider using the high-tech look of the shadowed effect. In a form formatted in the Stone style, consider using the etched or chiseled effects.

Apply a Special Effect to a Control

1 Display the form or report in Design view.

2 Select the control to which you want to apply a special effect.

3 Click the Special Effect drop-down arrow on the Formatting toolbar, and then click the effect you want to use.

Note that only the control's line or border is affected. Any text in the control is not affected by applying a special effect.

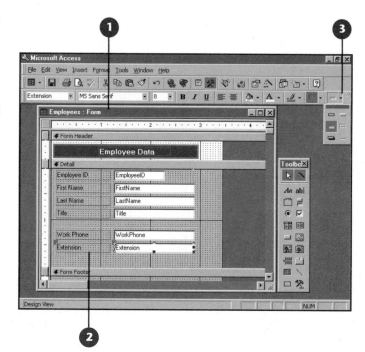

12

Adding Graphics to Forms and Reports

To further ehance your database forms and reports, you can add graphics from many sources. Microsoft Access 97 allows you to insert information, such as Microsoft Graph charts, or Microsoft Excel worksheet and charts, into database forms and reports. *Microsoft Graph* lets you create charts using data from database tables or queries. *Microsoft Excel* is a spreadsheet program that lets you record, analyze, and present information.

Object Linking and Embedding

In Access, you can insert an object created in another program into a presentation using a program-integration technology known as *Object Linking and Embedding* (OLE). OLE is an important feature for many Access users because with it you can create a form or report that draws on information from any program that uses the technology—and these days, most Windows programs do. When you share objects using OLE, the menus and toolbars from the program that created the object are available to you from within your form or report. You can edit inserted information without having to leave Access.

Sharing Information Among Documents

One of the great technological steps forward recently in personal computing has been the ability to insert an object created in one program into a document created in another program. Terms that you'll find useful in understanding how you can share objects among documents include:

TERM	DEFINITION
source program	The program that created the original object.
source file	The file that contains the original object.
destination program	The program that created the document into which you are inserting the object.
destination file	The file into which you are inserting the object.

For example, if you place an Excel chart in your PowerPoint presentation, Excel is the source program and PowerPoint is the destination program. The chart is the source file; the presentation is the destination file.

There are three ways to share information in Windows programs: pasting, embedding, and linking.

Pasting

You can cut or copy an object from one document and then paste it into another using the Cut, Copy, and Paste buttons on the source and destination program toolbars.

Embedding

When you *embed* an object, you place a copy of the object in the destination file, and when you activate the object, the tools from the source program become available in your presentation. For example, if you insert an Excel chart into your PowerPoint presentation, the Excel menus and toolbars become available, replacing the PowerPoint menus and toolbars, so you can edit the chart if necessary. With embedding, any changes you make to the chart in the presentation do not affect the original file.

Linking

When you *link* an object, you insert a representation of the object itself into the destination file. The tools of the source program are available, and when you use them to edit the object you've inserted, you are actually editing the source file. Moreover, any changes you make to the source file are reflected in the destination file.

Copying and Pasting Objects

When you copy or cut an object, Windows temporarily stores the object in an area in your computer's active memory, called the *Clipboard*. You can paste the object into the destination file using the Paste button or the Paste Special command, which gives you more control over how the object will appear in the destination file.

TIP

Be careful of file size when pasting objects. *When you click Paste, you are sometimes actually embedding. Because embedding can greatly increase file size, you might want to use Paste Special if disk space is at a premium. You can select a format that requires minimal disk space, pasting the object as a simple picture or simple text instead of as an embedded object.*

Paste an Object

1 Select the object in the source program.

2 Click the Copy button on the source program's toolbar.

3 Switch to Access and display the form or report on which you want to paste the object.

4 Click the Paste button on the Standard toolbar.

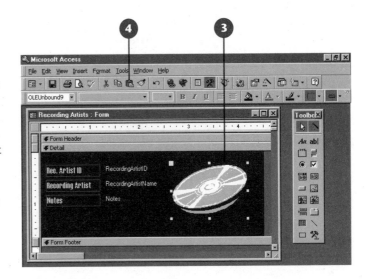

Paste Information in a Specified Format

1 Select the object in the source program.

2 Click the Copy button on the source program's toolbar.

3 Switch to Access and display the form or report on which you want to paste the object.

4 Click the Edit menu, and then click Paste Special.

5 Click the object type you want in the As list box.

6 Click OK.

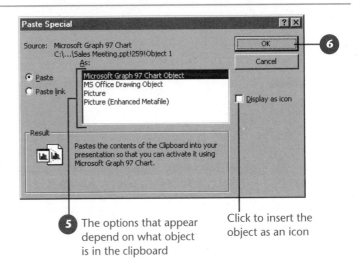

5 The options that appear depend on what object is in the clipboard

Click to insert the object as an icon

12

Inserting a New Object

If you don't already have an existing file to insert in a report or form, you create a new graphic from scratch without leaving the Access program. After you drag to create new Unbound Object Frame control, the Insert Object dialog box appears. You select the program in which you want to create the graphic. For example, if you want to create a picture in Microsoft Paint, which is provided with Windows 95, double-click Paint. If you want to use WordArt to create special text effects, such as creative text for a custom logo, double-click WordArt 3.0. The programs you see in this dialog box are the programs installed on your computer in which you can create graphics.

Create a New Graphic to Insert

1. Display the form or report in Design view.

2. Click the Unbound Object Frame button on the Toolbox.

3. With the Unbound Object pointer, drag a rectangle where you want the picture to appear. Make the rectangle approximately the same size as the picture you will insert.

4. Release the mouse button.

5. In the Insert Object dialog box, click the Create New option button.

6. Double-click the program in which you want to create a graphic or text effect object.

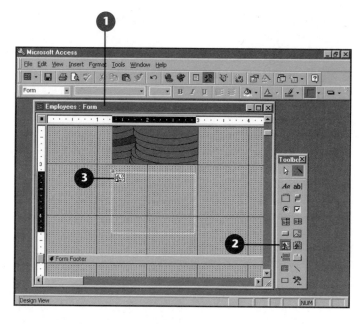

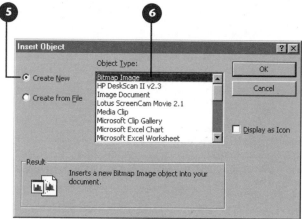

Consult your program's documentation or Help system. *To learn more about creating graphics or special text effects, consult the documentation or Help system provided with your graphics program.*

Edit the original graphic. *Double-click the graphic object you created to re-display the program in which you created the object, and then modify the graphic as necessary. When you close the program, the modified graphic will be inserted in the form or report.*

7 In the window or dialog box of the program you chose, create and save the graphic image.

8 Close the window or dialog box to return to Access, and insert the graphic you created.

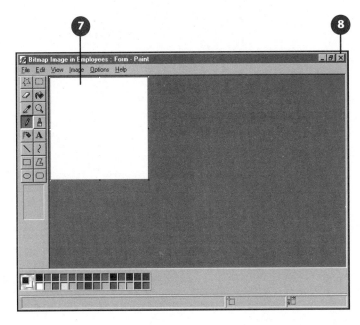

12

Inserting an Object from a File

There are several ways to embed or link an object to a slide. If you are creating a new object from scratch, you can use the Insert Object command. If you want to insert an existing file, you can also use Insert Object and you can specify whether or not you want to link the object. If your object is already open in the program that created it, you can copy it, and in some cases, paste it into a form or report, automatically embedding it. Finally, you can use the Paste Special command to paste link a copied object— pasting and linking it at the same time.

Insert a File

1 Click the Insert menu.

2 Click Object.

3 Click the Create From File option button.

4 Click the Browse button.

5 Click the Look In drop-down arrow, select the file location, select the file you want to insert, and then click Open.

6 To embed the object, make sure the Link check box is not checked. To link it, click the Link check box to select it.

7 Click OK.

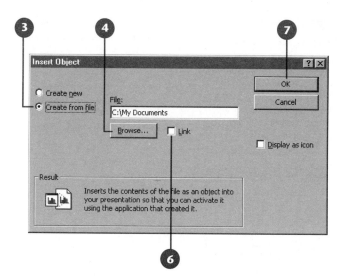

Paste Link an Object

1. In the source program, select the object you want to paste link.

2. Click the Cut or Copy button on the Standard toolbar in the source program.

3. Switch to your database form or report.

4. Click the Edit menu, and then click Paste Special.

5. Click the Paste Link option button.

6. Click the format you want.

7. Click OK.

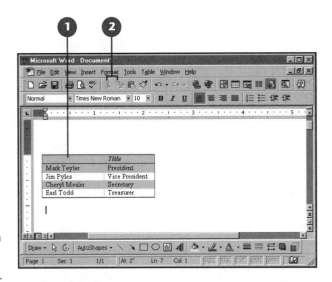

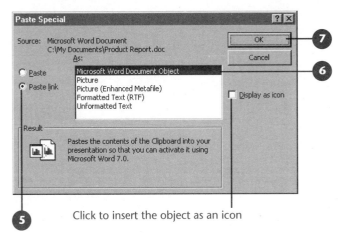

Click to insert the object as an icon

Inserting a Picture

For maximum visual impact in a report or form, you can add graphics to support the text or to provide visual interest. You can choose to insert a graphics file that has already been created or that is part of the Office 97 clip art collection. You can also create a new graphic in the graphics program of your choice, and then add it to a form or report.

Image button

Insert a Graphics File

1. Display the form or report in Design view.

2. Click the Image button on the Toolbox.

3. With the image pointer, drag a rectangle where you want the picture to appear. Make the rectangle approximately the same size as the picture you will insert.

4. Release the mouse button.

5. In the Insert Picture dialog box, locate the folder containing the picture you want to insert. For example, if you want to insert a picture from the clip art collection provided with Office, open the Clipart folder in the Office folder.

6. Double-click the file you want to insert.

   The graphic now appears in the report or form.

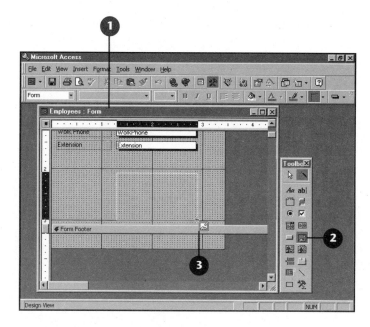

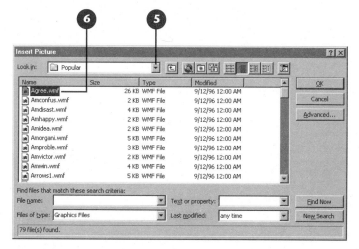

Cut (crop) away parts of a graphic that you want to hide. *Place the pointer over a sizing handle and hold down the Shift key as you drag in the direction you want to go. For example drag toward the center of the graphic to crop out the parts you don't want to see. To create more space around the graphic, drag away (while holding down the Shift key) from the center of the graphic.*

7 Size the graphic as needed by dragging the sizing handles.

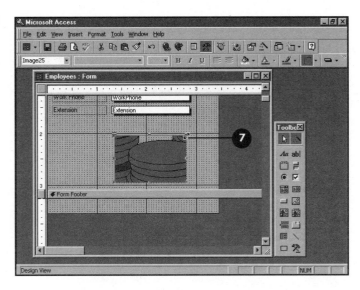

12

Inserting Clip Art

You can add clip art, copyright-free graphics, to a form or report. Your company might have a logo that it includes in all forms and reports. You can also add clip art or pictures to a field. For example, in an employee table you can have a field that contains an image file that is a photo of the employee. Or you might have a field containing a Word document that is a recent performance review. When you run a report that includes this field, you will see the contents of the field. In Datasheet view, you can double-click the field to display the field's contents.

Insert a Clip Art Object

1. Position the insertion point in the form, report, or field.

2. Click the Insert menu, and then click Object.

3. Click the Create New option button to display a list of object types you can insert.

4. Click Microsoft Clipart Gallery, and then click OK.

5. Click the Clip Art tab.

6. Click the category you want.

7. Click the clip art graphic you want to insert.

8. Click Insert to insert the graphic and return to your table.

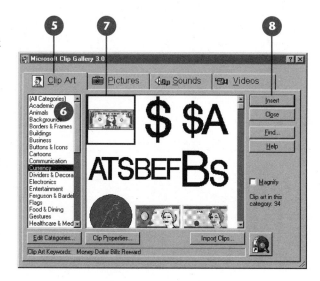

Moving and Resizing an Object

After you insert a graphic object, you can resize or move it with its selection *handles*, the little squares that appear on the edge of the object when you click the object to select it.

SEE ALSO

See "Sizing Tables" on page 23 for more information on resizing windows.

Move an Object

1. Select an object you want to move.

2. Position the mouse pointer (which changes to a hand) over the object, and then click and drag the pointer to move the outline of the object to a new location. (Do not click a handle or you will resize the object.)

3. Release the mouse button.

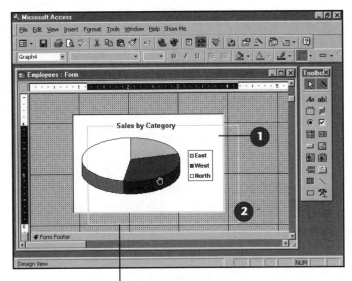

Outline indicates new position.

Resize an Object

1. Select an object you want to resize.

2. Position the mouse pointer over one of the handles.

3. Drag the handle to the size you want the object to be.

4. Release the mouse button.

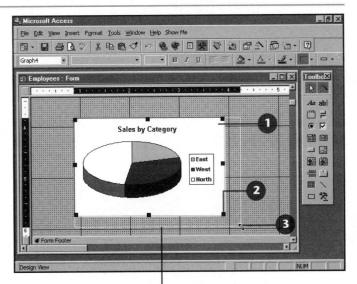

Outline indicates new chart size.

Inserting Excel Charts and Worksheets

There are several types of Excel objects that you can insert into your form or report. Two of the most common are worksheets and charts. You can insert a new Excel worksheet and then add data to it, or you can insert an existing Excel worksheet. You can also insert a chart from an Excel workbook.

TIP

Use drag-and-drop to insert a chart. *Open both Excel and Access, select the chart in Excel, and then drag it into Access. Press Ctrl while you drag to copy the chart.*

SEE ALSO

See "Inserting a Graph Chart" on page 172 for information on inserting a chart using Microsoft Graph.

Insert an Existing Excel Chart

1. Open the worksheet containing the chart in Excel.

2. Click the chart, and then click the Copy button on Excel's Standard toolbar.

3. Switch to Access and the form or report on which you want the chart.

4. Click the Paste button on the Standard toolbar.

5. Click outside the chart to deselect it.

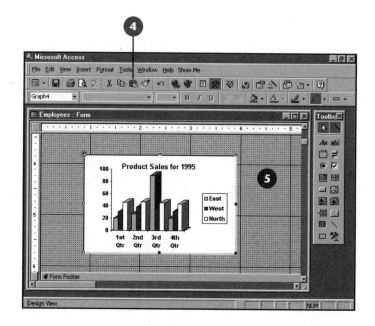

Display only a certain portion of a worksheet.
Double-click the embedded Excel object, and then drag the sizing handles until only the rows and columns you want are displayed. You can also use the Crop tool on the Picture toolbar to crop unwanted portions.

Insert Data Stored in an Excel Worksheet

1. Display the form or report on which you want to insert the Excel worksheet.

2. Click the Insert menu, and then click Object.

3. Click the Create From File option button, click the Browse button, and then locate and select the worksheet you want. Click OK.

4. To link the worksheet, click the Link check box.

5. Click OK.

6. Double-click the worksheet object to edit the data.

7. If necessary, edit the worksheet using the Excel tools.

8. Click the File menu, and then click Exit.

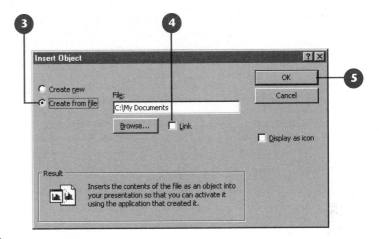

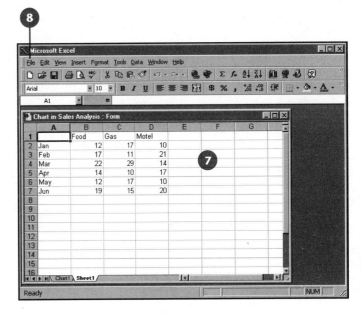

Inserting a Map

Data for geographic locations can be charted using any existing chart type, but you can add real impact by using Excel's special mapping feature. This mapping feature analyzes and charts your data in an actual geographic map containing countries or states and helps readers understand the relationship of geographic data when viewed within a map. For example, seeing population data displayed within a map of the United States would probably have more meaning for you than to see the same information displayed in a column chart.

SEE ALSO

See "Modifying a Map" on page 171 for more information on about changing a map.

Create a Geographic Map

1 Display the form or report in Design view, click the Insert menu, and then click Object.

2 Click Microsoft Map, and then click OK.

3 In the Map window, click the Insert menu on, and then click External Data.

4 Click Microsoft Access, and then Click OK.

5 In the Open Database dialog box, double-click the databse you want to use.

6 Select the fields in the table to display in the map, and then click Add (>) to include the each field.

7 Click OK.

8 Select a map template, if necessary, and then click OK.

9 Click the File menu, and then click Exit & Return to ... [Form or Report].

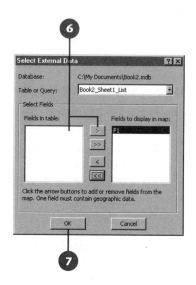

Modifying a Map

An existing geographic map can be modified to reflect updated data. You must update the geographic map when you change the data. In addition, the colors and patterns used to display the data within the map can also be changed.

TIP

Always refresh a map after changing database data. *Unlike chart data, Access does not automatically update map data whenever data changes.*

SEE ALSO

See "Moving and Resizing a Object" on page 167 for information about moving and resizing a map.

Modify a Geographic Map

1. Display the form or report where the map is located.

2. Double-click the map.

3. If necessary, click the Map Refresh button on the Microsoft Map toolbar.

4. Change data and the way it is displayed in the map using buttons in the Microsoft Map Control dialog box. Press Esc to deselect the map.

5. Click the File menu, and then click Exit & Return to ... [Form or Report].

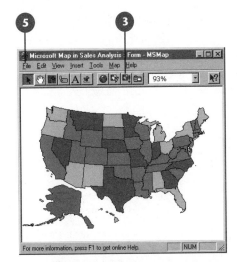

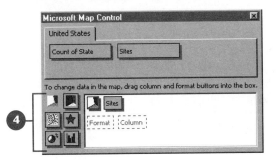

12

Inserting a Graph Chart

You can create a chart from scratch using the graph program that comes with the Office 97 suite, *Microsoft Graph*. Graph uses two views to display the information that makes up a graph: the *datasheet*, a spreadsheet-like grid of rows and columns that contains your data, and the *chart*, the graphical representation of the data.

A datasheet contains cells to hold your data. A *cell* is the intersection of a row and column. A group of data values from a row or column of data makes up a *data series*. Each data series has a unique color or pattern on the chart.

Create a Graph Chart

1 Display the form or report in Design view.

2 Click the Insert menu, and then click Chart.

If a message dialog box appears asking you to install an advanced wizard, use your setup program to install the chart wizard.

3 Drag the size of the chart you want to create.

4 In the View area, click the Both option, and then click a table or query.

5 Click Next.

6 Click each field you want to chart, and then click Add (>) button to include the field.

7 When you are done adding fields, click Next.

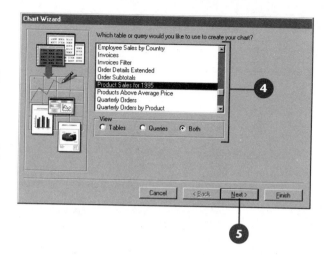

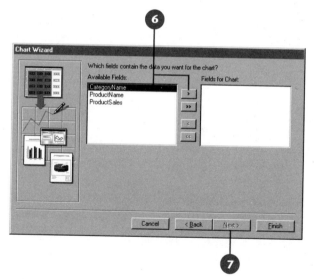

SEE ALSO

See "Selecting a Chart Type" on page 174 for information on selecting a different chart type.

8 Click a chart type.

9 Click Next.

10 Click the Preveiw Chart button, and then click Close after viewing the chart.

11 Click Next.

12 Enter a chart title, if necessary, or select fields to point in the chart, if necessary, and then click Next.

13 Click Finished to create a chart in Access.

14 Click the File menu, and then click Exit & Return to ... [Form or Report].

15 To open the chart, double-click the chart.

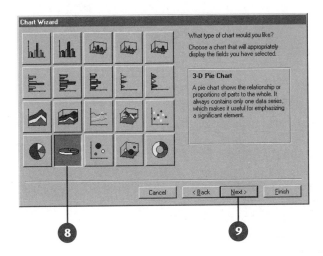

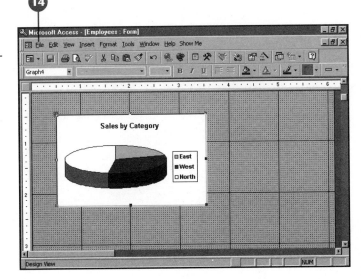

Selecting a Chart Type

Your chart is what your audience will see, so make sure to take advantage of Access' chart formatting options. You start by choosing the chart type you want. There are 18 chart types, available in 2-D and 3-D formats, and for each chart type you can choose from a variety of formats. If you want to format your chart beyond the provided formats, you can customize any chart object to your own specifications and can then save those settings so that you can apply that chart formatting to any chart you create.

Select a Chart Type

1 In Graph, click the View Datasheet button on the Graph toolbar, if neccesary, to view the chart.

2 Click the Chart Type drop-down arrow on the Standard toolbar.

3 Click the button corresponding to the chart type you want.

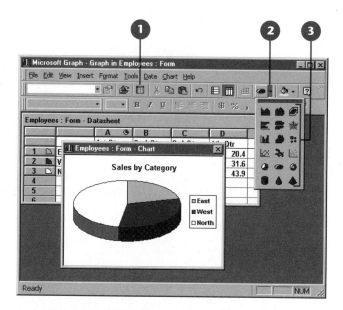

Apply a Standard Chart Type

1 Click the Chart menu, and then click Chart Type.

2 Click the Standard Types tab.

3 Click the chart type you want.

4 Click the chart sub-type you want. *Sub-types* are variations on the chart type.

5 Click OK.

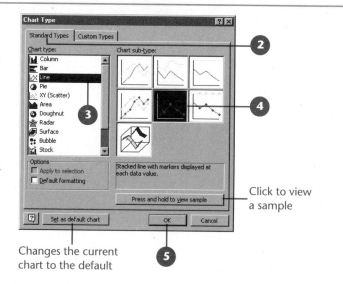

Click to view a sample

Changes the current chart to the default

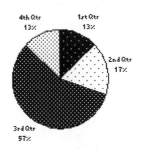

Apply a Custom Chart Type

1. Click the Chart menu, and then click Chart Type.

2. Click the Custom Types tab.

3. Click the Built-in option button.

4. Click the chart type you want.

5. Click OK.

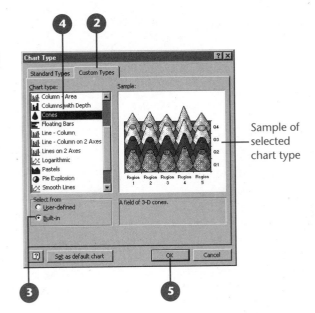

Sample of selected chart type

"I put a lot of work into creating this chart—how can I save the formatting to apply to other charts?"

Create a Custom Chart Type

1. Click the Chart menu, and then click Chart Type.

2. Click the Custom Types tab.

3. Click the User-defined option button.

4. Click Add.

5. Type a name and description for the chart.

6. Click OK twice.

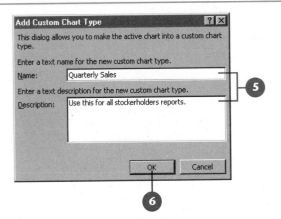

12

Editing Graph Data

Although most of the time you edit Microsoft Graph data in the datasheet, you can change it in the chart by dragging a data marker. This method is easy, but it's hard to be accurate, and only works for 2-D charts, 3-D charts. You can edit data one cell at a time, or you can manipulate blocks of adjacent data called *ranges*. If you are familiar with electronic spreadsheets, you will find Microsoft Graph uses many of the same data editing techniques.

Edit Cell Contents

1 Double-click the chart you want to edit in a form or report.

2 Click the Dataview button, if necessary, to view the datasheet.

3 Click the cell you want to edit.

- ◆ To replace the cell contents, type the new data into the cell. It replaces the previous entry.

- ◆ To edit the cell contents, double-click the selected cell where you want to edit.

- ◆ Press the Delete and Backspace keys to delete one character at a time, and then type in the new data.

4 Click the File menu, and then click Exit & Return to ... [Form or Report].

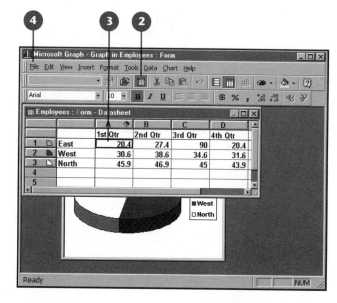

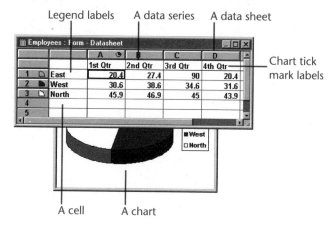

Legend labels   A data series   A data sheet

Chart tick mark labels

A cell   A chart

13

Accessing the Internet

World Wide Web technology is now available in Access databases. For better productivity and easier compilation of information, you can add *hyperlinks* (graphic or text objects you click to jump to other documents and intranet or Internet pages) within your Access databases.

Once you click several hyperlinks, opening several documents, you need a way to move between these open documents. The Web toolbar makes this simple with its Web-like navigation tools. You can move backward or forward one document at a time or jump to any document with just a couple of mouse clicks.

Whether a document is stored on your computer, network, intranet, or across the globe, you can access it from Access. Just display the Web toolbar and you're ready to jump to any document, no matter where it resides. With the Web toolbar search capabilities, you can search for information on the Web, and then enter it into an Access database. If you find a document that you want to visit again, you can add it to a list of favorites documents to revisit later.

With Access, you can publish a database on the Web for others to view using a Web browser. To publish the Internet ready document, Access uses ActiveX controls.

Inserting Hyperlinks in Forms and Reports

Sometimes, you'll want to refer to another part of an Access form, table, or report, or even to a file created in another program. Rather than duplicating the material or adding a note, you can create a *hyperlink*, which is a colored, underlined label, picture, or command button you click to move (or *jump*) to a new location within the same file or to a location in another file on your computer or network, or to a Web page on your intranet or the Internet. You can insert a hyperlink directly on a form or report only.

Insert Hyperlink button

Create a Hyperlink Within a Database

1 Open a form or report in Design view.

2 Click the Insert Hyperlink button on the toolbar.

3 Click the Named Location In File Browse button, and then double-click the database object you want to jump to.

4 Click OK twice.

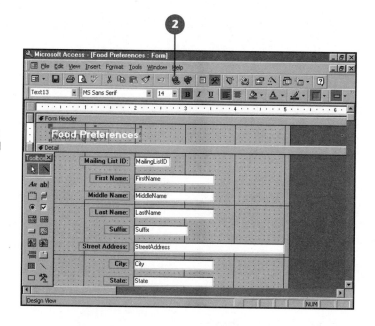

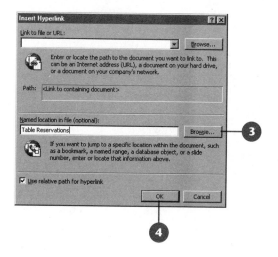

TIP

Internet Addresses and URLs. *Every Web page has a uniform resource locator (URL), an Internet address in a form your browser program can decipher. Like postal addresses and e-mail addresses, each URL contains specific parts that identify where a Web page is located. For example, the URL for Microsoft's Web page is http://www.microsoft.com/, where "http://" indicates the address is on the Web and "www.microsoft.com" indicates the name of the computer or network server on which the Web page is stored.*

TIP

Remove a hyperlink. *To remove a hyperlink from your database, open the form or report that contains the hyperlink in Design view. Right-click the hyperlink, and then click Cut on the shortcut menu.*

TIP

Hyperlinks in reports. *Although you can add hyperlinks to an Access report, the hyperlink will work only when you publish the report to Word, Excel, or HTML.*

Insert a Hyperlink to Another File or URL

1. Open a form or report in Design view.

2. Click the Insert Hyperlink button on the toolbar.

3. Click the Link To File Or URL Browse button, and then double-click the name of the file you want to jump to; or type a URL in the Link To File Or URL box.

4. Click OK.

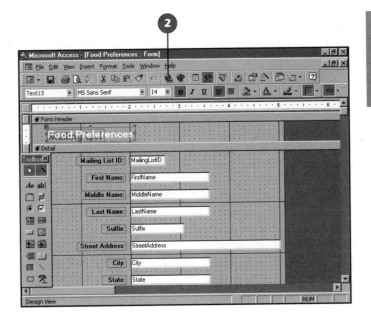

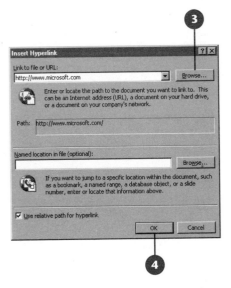

Inserting Hyperlinks in Table Fields

Besides inserting hyperlinks directly on a form or report, you can insert a hyperlink within a table. To insert a hyperlink within a table, you must define a field with the data type Hyperlink, which can be a path to a file on your hard drive, or a URL. When you click on a hyperlink field, Access jumps to an object, document, World Wide Web page, or other destination.

SEE ALSO

See "Inserting Hyperlinks in Forms and Reports" on page 178 for more information about hyperlinks.

Create a Hyperlink Field in a Table

1. Open a table in Design view.

2. Create a new field in which you will store hyperlinks.

3. Click the Data Type drop-down arrow, and then click Hyperlink.

4. Click the Save button on the Tables Design toolbar.

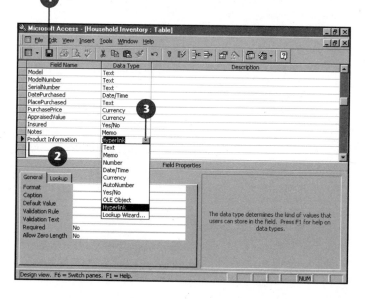

Using the Web Toolbar

The Web toolbar makes it easy to navigate hyperlinked files. While you explore, you can hide other toolbars to gain the most screen space.

Web Toolbar button

Show Only Web Toolbar button

SEE ALSO

See "Navigating Hyperlinks" on page 184 for more information about using the buttons on the Web Toolbar.

Display or Hide the Web Toolbar

1. Open the table, query, or form you want to work with, or display the report you want to work with in Design view.

2. Click the Web Toolbar button on the toolbar.

3. Click the Show Only Web Toolbar button on the Web toolbar.

4. To redisplay other toolbar, click the Show Only Web Toolbar button again.

5. To hide the Web toolbar, click the Web Toolbar button again.

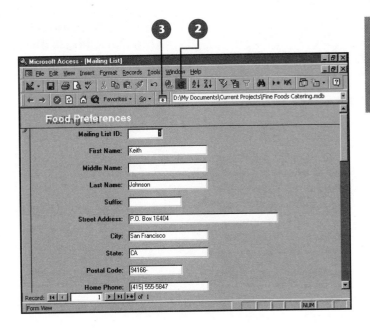

Jumping to Hyperlinked Documents

You can jump directly to a document on your computer or network, or to a Web page on your intranet or the Internet using the Web toolbar. In the Address box on the Web toolbar, type the address to the document you want to view and press Enter. To jump to a document on your hard drive or network, enter its filename (including its path, for example, C:\My Documents\Memos\To Do List.doc). To jump to a Web document, enter its Internet address (a URL, for example, http://www.microsoft.com).

Jump to a Document Using the Address Box

1. Click the Address box on the Web toolbar to select the current address.

2. Type an address to the document. For example, C:\My Documents \Memos\Fall 1997 Seminars Memo.doc. The address includes:

   ◆ A hard drive (C:\)

   ◆ One or more folders (My Documents \Memos)

   ◆ A filename (Fall 1997 Seminars Memo.doc)

3. Press Enter.

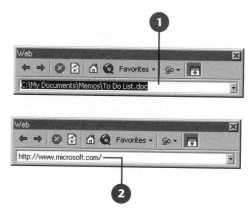

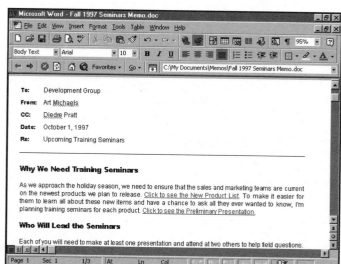

Open a Web document. *In the Address box, enter the complete location of the document you want to open, including the computer drive, filename, and file extension. If you have access to the Internet, you can enter a URL for a Web page.*

See "Inserting Hyperlinks in Forms and Reports" on page 178 for more information about Internet addresses and URLs.

Jump to a Web Document Using the Address Box

1 Click the Address box on the Web toolbar to select the current address.

2 Type an Internet address. For example, http://www.microsoft.com (Microsoft's Web address).

3 Press Enter.

4 Connect to the Internet through your Internet Service Provider (ISP) or network. Your Web browser opens (such as Microsoft Internet Explorer).

5 Click any hyperlink to explore the Web site.

6 When you are finished, click the File menu, and then click Close.

7 If necessary, click Yes to disconnect from the Internet.

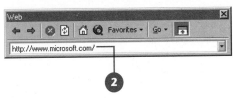

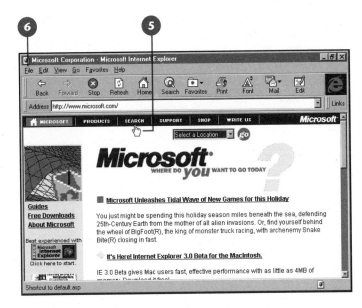

Navigating Hyperlinks

As you explore hyperlinked documents, you might want to retrace your steps and return to a document you've already visited. You can move backward and then forward one document at a time, or you can jump directly to any document from the *Address list*, which shows the last 10 documents you've linked to. This way you can quickly jump to any document without having to click through them one by one. After you start the jump to a document, you can stop the link if the document opens (or *loads*) slowly or you decide not to access it. If a document loads incorrectly or you want to update the information it contains, you can reload, or *refresh*, the page. You can make any document your *start page*, or home base. Set your start page to a document you want to access quickly and frequently.

Back Up One Document

1 Click the Back button on the Web toolbar.

Move Forward One Document

1 Click the Forward button on the Web toolbar until you return to the most recent document you opened.

The Back button dims when you reach the first document you opened.

Jump to Any Open Hyperlinked Document

1 Click the Address drop-down arrow.

2 Click the document you want.

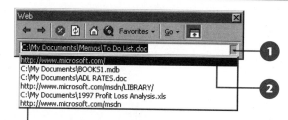

The address list shows all the documents you've opened this session, in the order you opened them.

Stop Current Jump button

Refresh Current Page button

Start Page button

SEE ALSO

See "Inserting Hyperlinks in Forms and Reports" on page 178 and see "Inserting Hyperlinks in Table Fields" on page 180 for more information about inserting hyperlinks.

Stop a Link

1 Click the Stop Current Jump button on the Web toolbar.

Reload a Document

1 Click the Refresh Current Page button on the Web toolbar.

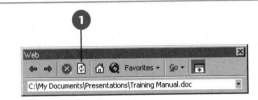

Jump to Your Start Page

1 Click the Start Page button on the Web toolbar.

Change Your Start Page

1 Open the document you want as your start page.

2 Click the Go button on the Web toolbar.

3 Click Set Start Page.

4 Click Yes to confirm the new start page.

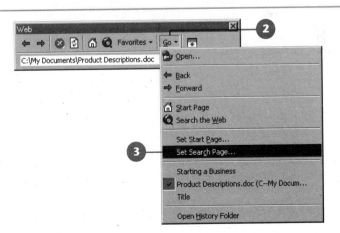

Searching for Information on the Web

You can find all kinds of information on the Web. The best way to find information is to use a search engine. A search engine allows you to search through a collection material to find what you are looking for. There are many search engines available on the Web, such as Yahoo! and Excite. You can make any document your *search page*. Set your search page to a reliable search engine you want to access frequently.

Search for Information on the Web

1. Click the Search the Web button on the Web toolbar.

2. Connect to the Internet through your Internet Service Provider (ISP) or network. Your Web browser opens (such as Microsoft Internet Explorer).

3. Type in a topic you want to find information on the Internet.

4. Select a search engine.

5. Click the Search button to start the search.

6. When you are finished, click the File menu, and then click Close.

7. If necessary, click Yes to disconnect from the Internet.

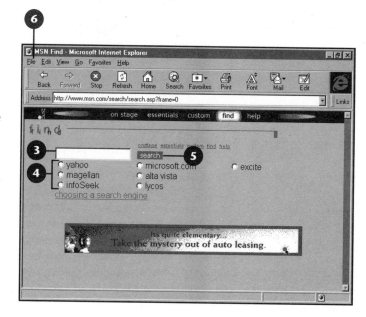

Use Office 97 File Viewers to display files. *File viewers allow anyone to view and print documents created in Word, Excel, and PowerPoint just as you would from within the programs even if they don't own the programs. You can download the viewers for free from Microsoft Corporation's Web site located at* **http://microsoft.com/msoffice/** *and send them to anyone who needs to look at your Word, Excel, and PowerPoint files.*

Change Your Search Page

1 Open the document you want as your search page.

2 Click the Go button on the Web toolbar.

3 Click Set Search Page.

4 Click Yes to confirm the new search page.

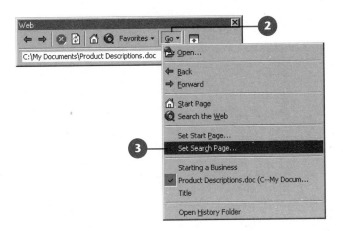

You can use any document, including an intranet or Web page, as your start page.

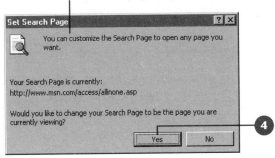

Returning to Favorites

When you have jumped to a document that you would like to return to in the future, you can add the document to a list of favorites. The Favorites button provides shortcuts to files you explore frequently so you won't need to retype long file locations. These shortcuts can open documents on your computer, network, Intranet, and the Internet.

Add a File Shortcut to Your Favorites Folder

1. Open the file you want to access from the Favorites folder.

2. Click the Favorites button on the Web toolbar.

3. Click Add To Favorites.

4. Type a new name if you want.

5. Click Add.

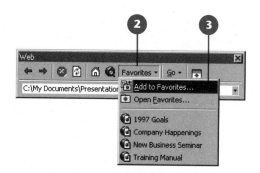

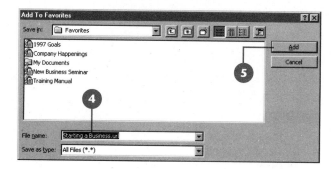

Jump to a Favorite Document

1. Click the Favorites button on the Web toolbar.

2. Click the document you want.

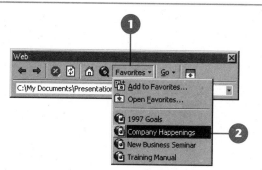

Getting Media Clips from the Web

You can find and download additional clip art, pictures, sounds, and videos from the Web into Microsoft Clip Gallery. With a click of a button, you can connect to the Web (through your browser), find graphic and multimedia files, and then download them into the Microsoft Clip Gallery.

Connect To Web For Additional Clips

SEE ALSO

See "Inserting Clip Art" on page 166 for more information about inserting clip art, pictures, sounds, and videos from the Microsoft Clip Gallery.

Get Additional Clips from the Web

1. Click the Insert menu, point to Picture, and then click Clip Art.

2. Click the Connect To Web For Additional Clips button. Your Web browser opens (such as Microsoft Internet Explorer).

3. Connect to the Internet through your Internet Service Provider (ISP) or network.

4. If necessary, click the Accept button, and then click Browse.

5. Click the media type you want: Clip Art, Pictures, Sounds, or Videos.

6. Click the Select A Category drop-down list arrow and then click the category you want.

7. Click Go.

8. When you are finished, click the File menu, and then click Close.

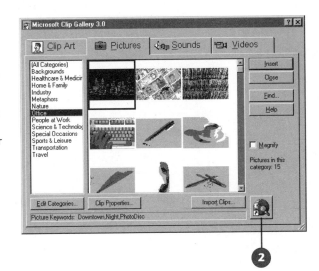

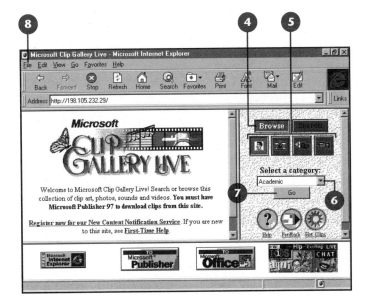

Inserting ActiveX Controls

ActiveX controls, new to Access 97, are objects you add to an Access form to improve its effectiveness and performance. Access 97 comes with a variety of controls, such as a Calendar control. You can also install, or *register*, other ActiveX controls that you purchase separately. You use an ActiveX Server when you publish a database or database object to the World Wide Web.

Register ActiveX Controls

1 If necessary, copy the files to your system for the new ActiveX control you want to register.

2 Click the Tools menu, and then click ActiveX Controls.

3 Click Register.

4 Switch to the folder where you copied the control files to your system.

5 Double-click the name of the control you want to register.

6 Click Close.

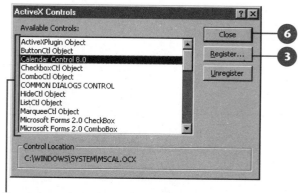

Shows the ActiveX controls currently registered on your system.

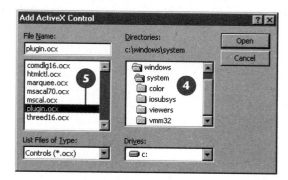

TIP

Controls in previous versions. *In previous versions of Access, ActiveX Controls were called custom controls and OLE controls.*

SEE ALSO

See "Publishing to the World Wide Web" on page 192 for information about using the ActiveX Server to publish on the Web.

Set ActiveX Server Options

1. Open the database in which you want to set the options, click the Tools menu, and then click Options.

2. Click the Hyperlinks/HTML tab.

3. Type the location of the server you want to use.

4. Type how long the server connection should be maintained without any activity.

5. Click OK.

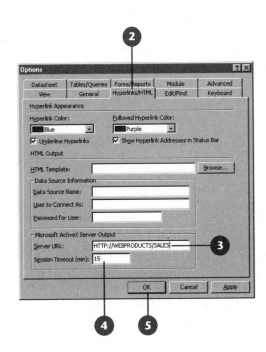

Publishing to the World Wide Web

HyperText Markup Language (HTML) is a simple coding system used to format documents for an intranet or the Internet. A Web browser program interprets these codes to determine how to display database objects. You can use the Publish To The Web Wizard to save datasheets, reports, or forms as HTML documents, ready to publish on the World Wide Web or on your intranet. A *static* HTML document shows the contents of an object at a particular moment, whereas a *dynamic* HTML document is updated with the latest information in your database each time someone accesses that Web page. When you create a dynamic format, Access creates an ActiveX Server Page.

Save Database Objects as HTML

1 Open the database containing the objects, click the File menu, and then click Save As HTML.

2 Read the information in the wizard window, and then click Next.

3 Select the tables, queries, forms, and reports you want to publish on the Web.

4 Click Next.

5 Follow the instructions in the Publish To The Web Wizard dialog box to set up the selected objects in HTML format.

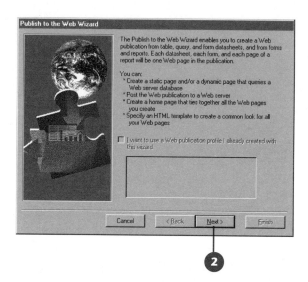

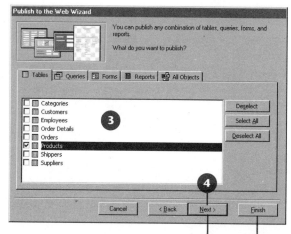

Click when you have completed a window.

Click when you have answered all the wizard's questions and are ready to publish the selected objects in HTML format.

Hyperlink colors. *A hyperlink changes color after the first time it has been clicked. To change the default colors, click the Tools menu, click Options, click the Hyperlinks/HTML tab, and then click the Hyperlink Color drop-down arrow, and then click a new color.*

See "Inserting ActiveX Controls" on page 190 for more information about ActiveX Server Pages.

Change HTML Options

1. Open the database in which you want to set the options, click the Tools menu, and then click Options.

2. Click the Hyperlinks/ HTML tab.

3. Click Browse, and then double-click the template you want to use as your default.

4. Enter Data Source Information.

5. Click OK.

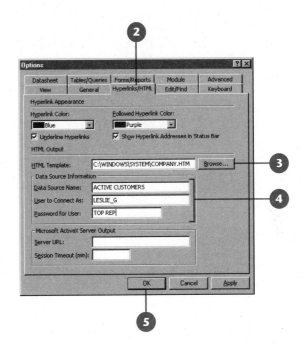

Accessing Microsoft on the Web

Because technology—not to mention people's needs—change so quickly, Microsoft has created their own World Wide Web site on the Internet. The site provides the most up-to-date information on Access as well as the latest templates and wizards. This is also the place to go if you need an answer to a technical problem or just want to read the most commonly requested information. If you are new to browsing the Web, try Microsoft's online tutorial to learn the basics about the World Wide Web. Also, let Microsoft know what you think about the company and its products.

TRY THIS

Get the latest templates. *If you have Internet access, check out the Free Stuff page on Microsoft's Web site. Download the latest templates available for Access 97.*

Get Help from Microsoft's World Wide Web Site

1. Make sure you have a modem and Internet access from your computer.

2. Click the Help menu, and then point to Microsoft On The Web.

3. Click the page of Microsoft's Web site you want.

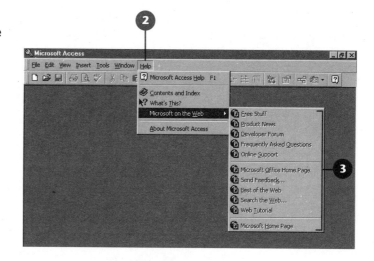

ACCESSING MICROSOFT ON THE WEB	
Web site	**Description**
Free Stuff	Download the latest Templates.
Product News	Find out What's new.
Developer Forum	Find Access developer information.
Frequently Asked Questions	Read the most commonly requested information.
Online Support	Get answers to your technical questions.
Office Home Page	Check out available services.
Send Feedback	Give Microsoft your comments.
Best of the Web	Check out highly rated Web sites.
Search the Web	Find the specific links and Web pages.
Web Tutorial	Learn how to use the World Wide Web.
Microsoft Home Page	Connect to Microsoft's Web Page.

Maximizing Database Performance

Once you're familiar with the basics of creating and using a database, you're ready to work with some of the more advanced features of Microsoft Access 97. For example, you can make your database more manageable by storing the data in multiple tables and then defining relationships between the tables so that you can work more efficiently.

Access also provides several tools to help you maximize your database's performance and ensure the integrity of the data stored in it. For example, you can analyze your database to ensure it is performing at its maximum efficiency. Then, you can repair the database as necessary. You can also secure your database by limiting who can open the database, specifying what objects they can work with and modify, and restricting what information they have access to. Additional Access tools enable you to copy a database, reduce the size of a database, and work with databases created in previous versions of Access.

Working with Multiple Tables

To work more efficiently with a database, you should organize records into several tables with fewer fields in each rather than in a single large table that contains all the fields you might ever need. With your data stored in multiple tables, you can expect to work in multiple tables at one time. By creating relationships between tables (based on fields the tables have in common), Access makes it easy to work with data stored in multiple tables. For example, you can create a query or report that displays data from more than one table. You can also create forms that store the information you enter into multiple tables. Once you have established table relationships, creating multiple-table objects is usually not much different from creating other objects that are based on only a single table. The wizard dialog boxes you use to create database objects always give you the opportunity to select fields from other tables in order to create multiple-table objects.

Building Table Relationships

With the Relationships feature in Access, you can create a relationship between tables. This relationship is based on a field that both tables have in common, called the *common field*. For example, a table that contains a Customer ID field can be related to another table that also contains a Customer ID field. In this case, the common field is the Customer ID field. Often the common field is the primary key in the first table,

which is referred to as the *primary table* in the relationship. The common field is known as the *foreign key* in the related table. You can establish relationships between as many tables as you want.

TABLE RELATIONSHIP TYPES	
Type	**Description**
One-to-one	Each record in the first table is related to only one record in the second table, and vice versa. This type of relationship is not common, because most data related in this way would be stored in the same table.
One-to-many	Each record in the first table (the *primary table*) is related to one or more records in the second table, and each record in the second table (the *related table*) is related to only one record in the first table. This is the most common type of relationship. For example, a one-to-many relationship would exist between a Customers table and an Orders table, because each customer could place multiple orders, but each order is placed for only one customer.
Many-to-many	Each record in the first table is related to multiple records in the second table, and each record in the second table is related to multiple records in the first table. To create this type of relationship between two tables, you must create a third table and form one-to-many relationships between it and each of the other two tables (in order to avoid data redundancy).

Understanding Referential Integrity

Referential integrity is a set of rules that Access enforces to maintain consistency between related tables when you update data in a database. These rules ensure that relationships between records in related tables are valid and that you don't accidentally delete or change related data. You can set referential integrity when:

◆ The common field from the primary table is a primary key.

◆ The related fields have the same data type.

◆ Both tables belong to the same database.

When referential integrity is enforced, you must observe the following rules:

◆ When you add a record to a related table, a matching record must already exist in the primary table.

◆ When you attempt to change the value of the primary key in the primary table, Access prevents this change if matching records exist in a related table.

◆ When you delete a record in the primary table, Access prevents the deletion if matching records exist in a related table.

If you want Access to enforce these rules, select the Enforce Referential Integrity check box when you create

the relationship. With referential integrity active, you see a message box informing you that the change is not allowed when you attempt an action that would break one of the rules.

You can ignore the rules against deleting or changing related records and still preserve referential integrity by clicking the Cascade Update Related Fields and Cascade Delete Related Records check boxes.

◆ When the Cascade Update Related Fields check box is selected, changing a primary key value in the primary table automatically updates the matching value in all related records.

◆ When the Cascade Delete Related Records check box is selected, deleting a record in the primary table deletes any related records in the related table.

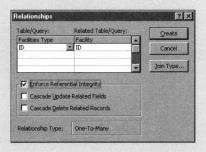

Defining Table Relationships

You can define table relationships in several ways. When you first create tables in your database using the Table Wizard, the wizard gives you an opportunity to define table relationships. You can also define relationships in the Database window or in Design view.

Insert Relationship button

Define Table Relationships

1. In the Database window, click the Relationships button on the Database toolbar.

   If relationships are already established in your database, you see them in the Relationships window. In this window you can create additional table relationships.

2. If necessary, click the Show Table button on the Relationship toolbar to display the Show Table dialog box.

3. Click the Tables tab.

4. Click the table you want.

5. Click Add.

   The table or query you selected appears in the Relationships window. Repeat steps 4 and 5 for each table you want to use in a relationship.

6. Click Close.

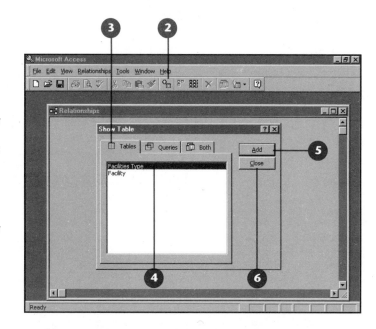

Tables related by a common field

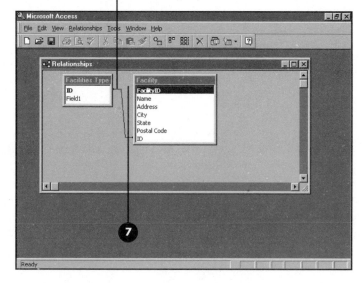

TIP

View the specific relation-ships you want to see. *Click the Show Direct Relationships button on the Relationship toolbar to see tables that are directly related to each other. Click the Show All Relation-ships button to see all the relationships between all the tables and queries in your database.*

TIP

Delete a table relation-ship. *In the Relationships window, select the line that joins the tables that you no longer want related to one another. Click the Edit menu, and then click Delete. In the message box, click Yes to confirm that you want to permanently delete this relationship. You will not be able to undo this change.*

7 Click the common field in the primary table and drag it to the common field in the related table. When you release the mouse button, a line appears between the two tables, signifying that they are related. Also, the Relationships dialog box opens, which allows you to confirm or modify the relationship.

8 Click the Join Type button, if you want to specify the join type. See the Join Types table for a complete description of each type. Click OK to return to the Relationships dialog box.

9 Click Create to create the relationship.

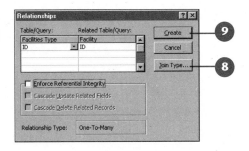

JOIN TYPES

Join Type	Description
Only include rows where the joined fields from both tables are equal.	Choose this option if you want to see one record in the second table for every record that appears in the first table. The number of records you see in the two tables will be the same.
Include ALL records from "xxx" (the first table) and only those records from "yyy" (the second table) where the joined fields are equal.	Choose this option if you want to see all the records in the first table (even if there is no corresponding record in the second table) as well as the records from the second table in which the joined fields are the same in both tables. The number of records you see in the first table might be greater than the number of records in the second table.
Include ALL records from "yyy" (the second table) and only those records from "xxx" (the first table) where the joined fields are equal.	Choose this option if you want to see all the records in the second table (even if there is no corresponding record in the first table) as well as the records from the first table in which the joined fields are the same in both tables. The number of records you see in the second table might be greater than the number of records in the first table.

Setting Up Accounts and Permissions

If many users work on the same database or a database contains confidential information, you might want to take extra steps to secure the database's structure or restrict access to specific information. You can do this by setting up accounts for groups or individuals and assigning permissions to them. A *group* is an account that contains individuals. *Permissions* limit the access that any account has to various objects and data in a database. By default, new accounts have full access to the database, and you'll need to remove permissions from them, as necessary, to create a secure database.

TIP

Admins group. *The Admins group is the system administrators' group account and has full permissions on all databases. You cannot delete it. To create and edit user accounts and permissions, you must log onto the system as a member of the Admins group.*

Create a User Account

1. Open the database for which you want to create the account.

2. Click the Tools menu, point to Security, and then click User And Group Accounts.

3. Click the Users tab.

4. Click New.

5. Type a name for the new account.

6. Type a personal identifier.

7. Click OK.

8. Click OK.

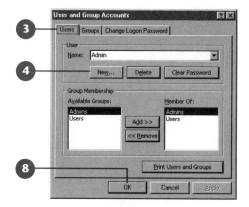

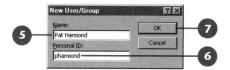

Change Account Permissions

1. Open the database for which you want to change permissions.

2. Click the Tools menu, point to Security, and then click User And Group Permissions.

3. Click the Permissions tab.

4. Click the Users option button or the Groups option button, depending on which account(s) you want to modify.

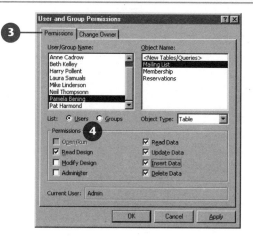

TIP

Personal Identifier. *Personal IDs contain between 4 and 20 letters (capitalization matters) or numbers or both. Along with the account name, a personal ID uniquely tags a user or group in a workgroup. Make sure you keep a copy of both the personal ID and account name in a secure location in case you need to retrieve an account that has been accidentally deleted or moved.*

TRY THIS

Simplify permissions management. *Instead of assigning permissions to individual users, assign permissions to groups and then add users to the appropriate groups. First, create a group for each permission level—click the Groups tab, click New, type a group name and personal ID, and then click OK. Second, assign different permissions to each group. Third, add users to each group.*

5. Click the name of the person or group for whom you want to change permissions.

6. Click the Object Type drop-down arrow, and then click an object type.

7. Click the name of an existing object or click <New Object>.

8. Click check boxes to add or remove permissions for the selected object.

9. Click Apply.

10. Click OK.

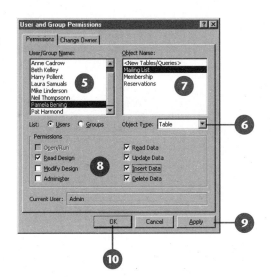

Delete a User Account

1. Open the database for which you want to delete a user account.

2. Click the Tools menu, point to Security, and then click User And Group Accounts.

3. Click the Users tab.

4. Click the Name drop-down arrow, and then click an account name.

5. Click Delete.

6. Click Yes to confirm the deletion, and then click OK.

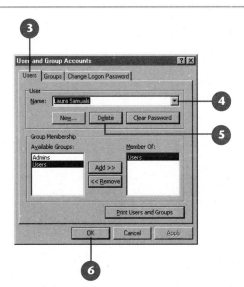

Securing a Database

Depending on how many users have access to your database or the sensitivity of the information it contains, you might want to prevent unauthorized users from opening the database by setting a password. Then each time someone tries to open the database, a dialog box appears requesting the password. Only those who enter the correct password can open the database. Another way to prevent unauthorized use of the database is to *encrypt it*. This compacts the database file and makes it indecipherable to a word processor or other programs. *Decrypting* a database reverses encrypting.

TIP

Remember your password!
Don't lose or forget the password you assign to a database because it cannot be recovered. If you forget your password, you won't be able to open the database.

Assign a Password to a Database

1. Make sure all users close the database, and then create a backup copy of the database.

2. Click the Open Database button on the Database toolbar.

3. Click the Exclusive check box to select it.

4. Double-click the database you want to protect.

5. Click the Tools menu, point to Security, and then click Set Database Password.

6. Type a password, and then press the Tab key.

7. Type the same password to verify it.

8. Click OK.

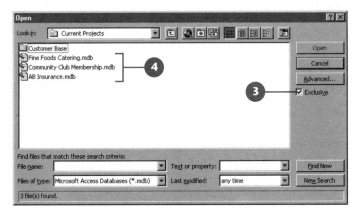

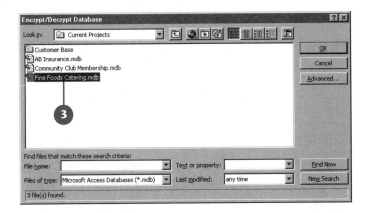

TIP

Do not assign a password for a replicated database. *If you plan to replicate a database, do not set a password for it. Replicated databases cannot be synchronized if database passwords are defined. If you link a table to a database with a password, the linked database might pick up the password.*

TIP

Close the database before encrypting. *A database must be closed to encrypt or decrypt it.*

TIP

Encryption does not restrict access. *Encryption does not affect whether someone has access to data or objects in a database. You must assign permissions to restrict access for specific users or groups.*

SEE ALSO

See "Customizing a Database Startup" on page 222 for information about how to set which menus and commands are available with a database.

Encrypt or Decrypt a Database

1 Close any open databases.

2 Click the Tools menu, point to Security, and then click Encrypt/Decrypt Database.

3 Double-click the database you want to encrypt or decrypt.

4 Click the Save In drop-down arrow, and then select the drive and folder in which you want to store the database.

5 Type a new name for the database.

6 Click Save.

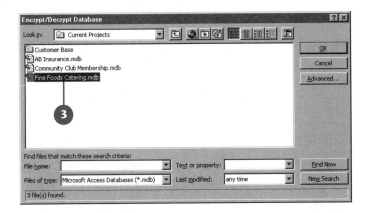

The dialog box title changes to Decrypt Database As when you decrypt a database rather than encrypt it.

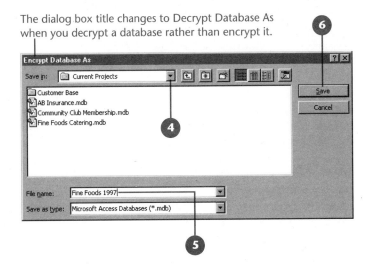

Reducing Database Size

When you delete database objects, such as tables, queries, or forms, the space occupied by the deleted objects in the database does not become available for other objects. To reclaim the space, you must *compact* the database, which creates a copy of the database and rearranges the data to fill in the spaces left by the deleted objects. The resulting database is smaller in size. You can also *split* a database, which places the tables in one file and the other database objects in another. This way, all the data remains in one place while each user can create their own forms, reports, and other objects based on their own needs. Splitting a database prevents it from becoming too large and unwieldy to work with efficiently.

Compact a Database

1. Close any open databases.

2. Click the Tools menu, point to Database Utilities, and then click Compact Database.

3. Double-click the database you want to compact.

4. Click the Save In drop-down arrow, and then select the drive and folder where you want to save the compacted database.

5. Type a new filename.

6. Click Save.

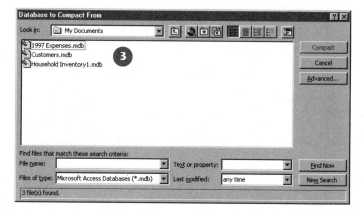

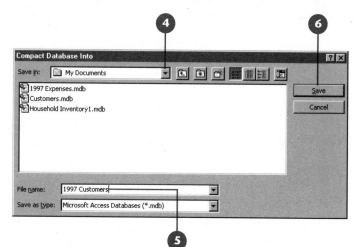

Split a Database

1 Open the database you want to split.

2 Click the Tools menu, point to Add-Ins, and then click Database Splitter.

3 Click Split Database.

4 Click the Save In drop-down arrow, and then select the drive and folder where you want to save the new database.

5 Type a new filename.

6 Click Split.

7 Click OK.

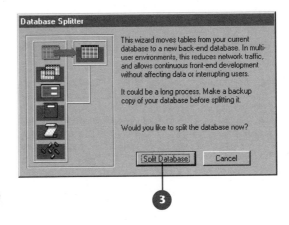

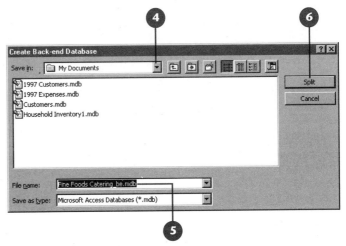

Replicating a Database

When users in different locations need to work with the same database, the best idea is to *replicate*, or copy, the database. The original database becomes the *Design Master*, the only version to which you can make structural changes. You can add, remove, or modify records in the Design Master or any replica (copy). Periodically, you should *synchronize*, or update, each replica with the Design Master to ensure that each file has the current data and database design. To resolve any conflict that arises when the same record is changed in the synchronized Design Master and replica, just choose which record you want to use.

SEE ALSO

See "Securing Your Database" on page 202 for information about database passwords.

Create a Replica

1. If necessary, remove the database password from the database.

2. Make sure you are the only user with the database open; all other users must close the database.

3. Click the Tools menu, point to Replication, and then click Create Replica.

4. Click Yes to close the database.

5. If necessary, click Yes to make a backup copy of the database.

6. Click the Save In drop-down arrow, and then select the drive and folder where you want to store the replica.

7. If necessary, type a new filename for the replica.

8. Click OK.

9. Click OK to confirm the message about the Design Master.

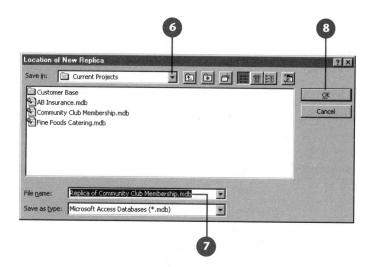

Replicate a database instead of sharing one copy over a network. *Replication helps to reduce network traffic because not everyone uses the same copy. You can also back up the Design Master while other users continue to work on their replicas.*

More about the Design Master. *The Design Master is a database to which system tables, fields, and replication properties are added. Only one Design Master exists per replica set.*

Synchronization and updates. *Synchronization exchanges updated records and objects between two replicas. The exchange can be one way or two way. If any replica is on the Internet, you'll get an additional dialog box when you synchronize, letting you choose whether you want to synchronize with someone on your network, intranet, or the Internet.*

Update a Replica

1 Open the replica you want to update.

2 Click the Tools menu, point to Replication, and then click Synchronize Now.

3 Click Browse, and then double-click the filename of the replica you want to update.

4 Click OK.

5 Click Yes to close and reopen the database.

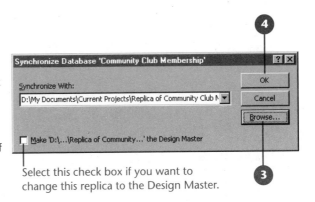

Select this check box if you want to change this replica to the Design Master.

Resolve Conflicts Between Replicas

1 Open the Design Master or the replica you want to check for conflict.

2 Click the Tools menu, point to Replication, and then click Resolve Conflicts.

3 Double-click a table name.

4 Click the button below the record you want to use.

5 Click Yes to confirm your choice.

6 Click OK.

7 Click Close.

Indicates the number of records with a conflict

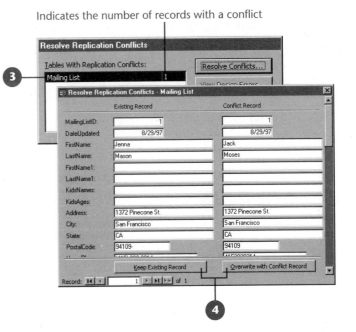

Repairing a Database

Access usually finds and repairs any damage when you open a database. Sometimes Access doesn't discover any problems, but you do! If your database begins to perform erratically, this can be a sign that something is wrong. Just run the Access repair utility to fix the damage.

TIP

Replace the original database with the repaired file. *Open the database you want to repair. Click the Tools menu, point to Database Utilities, and then click Repair Database. The repaired file replaces the original database.*

TRY THIS

Repair damage on your database. *Periodically, try using the Repair Database command to fix any undetected errors on your database.*

Repair a Database

1 Close any open databases.

2 Click the Tools menu, point to Database Utilities, and then click Repair Database.

3 Click the Look In drop-down arrow, and then select the drive and folder that contains the database you want to repair.

4 Double-click the database you want to repair.

5 Click OK.

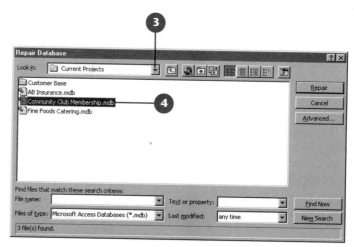

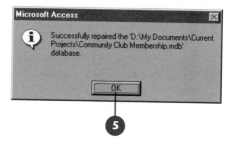

Adding Functionality with Add-Ins

Add-ins are programs that help you work with a program or perform a complex task more easily. Some add-ins, such as wizards, come with the program; you can also create and purchase other add-ins. In Access 97, use the *Add-In Manager* to install and remove add-ins. You might also want to use the *Linked Table Manager* to verify, and if needed, correct the filenames and locations of linked tables. The *Switchboard Manager* makes it simple to create a customized switchboard form.

Install and Uninstall Add-Ins

1. Open the database.

2. Click the Tools menu, point to Add-Ins, and then click Add-In Manager.

3. Click Add New, and then double-click the add-in you want to install.

4. Double-click any available add-in to install it.

5. Click any installed add-in you want to remove, and then click Uninstall.

6. Click Close.

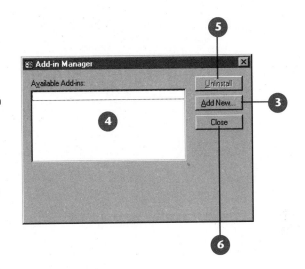

14

Using Add-Ins

Access comes with two add-ins: Linked Table Manager and Switchboard Manager. The *Linked Table Manager* allows you to verify, and if needed, correct the filenames and locations of linked tables. The *Switchboard Manager* makes it simple to create a customized switchboard form.

Update Linked Tables

1. Open the database.

2. Click the Tools menu, point to Add-Ins, and then click Linked Table Manager.

3. Click the check boxes for tables whose links you want to refresh.

4. Click OK.

5. If needed, double-click the filename of the database with the linked table.

6. Click OK to confirm all links are refreshed.

7. Click Close.

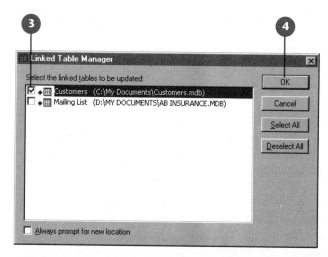

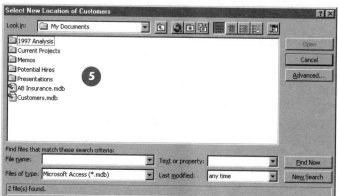

SEE ALSO

See "Customizing a Database Startup" on page 222 for information about displaying a switchboard form when you open a database.

"How can I create a switchboard for my database?"

Create a New Custom Switchboard Form

1. Open the database for which you want to create a switchboard.

2. Click the Tools menu, point to Add-Ins, click Switchboard Manager, and then click Yes to create a new switchboard.

3. Click New, type a name for the switchboard form, and then click OK.

4. Click the new switchboard name, and then click Edit.

5. Click New.

6. Type text for a switchboard button.

7. Click the Command drop-down arrow, and then click a command.

8. Click the Form drop-down arrow, and then click a form.

9. Click OK.

10. Repeat steps 5 through 9 for each button you want on the switchboard.

11. Click Close twice.

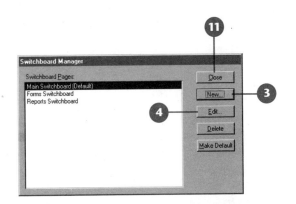

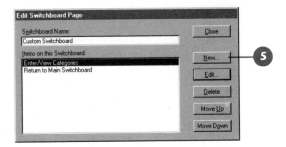

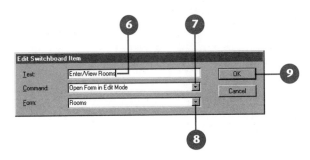

14

Using Previous-Version Access Databases

To give you the most flexibility when upgrading to Access 97, you can either convert or enable a database created in a previous version of Access. *Converting* permanently changes the format of the earlier version database to Access 97, allowing you to add, delete, or modify records, as well as redesign objects and use features available only in Access 97. *Enabling* opens the previous-version database in Access 97 and temporarily converts its objects and format so you can add, delete, or modify records. You can still open the database in the Access version in which it was created, and you must make design changes from the earlier version.

Convert a Database to Access 97

1 Close any open databases.

2 Click the Tools menu, point to Database Utilities, and then click Convert Database.

3 Click the Look In drop-down arrow, and then select the drive and folder that contain the database you want to convert.

4 Double-click the database you want to convert.

5 Click the Save In drop-down arrow, and then select the drive and folder where you want to store the converted database.

6 Type a new name for the database.

7 Click Save.

8 Open and work with the converted database with the usual Access 97 commands.

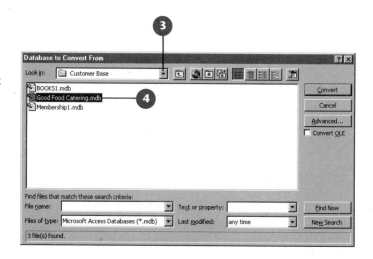

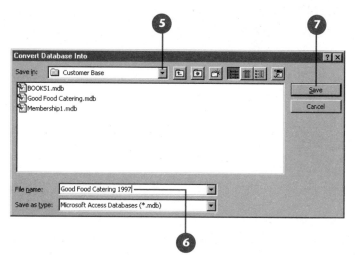

Enable a Database in Access 97

1. Click the Open Database button on the Database toolbar.

2. Click the Look In drop-down arrow, and then select the drive and folder that contains the database you want to enable.

3. Double-click the database you want to enable.

4. Click the Open Database option button.

5. Click OK.

6. Click OK to confirm your selection.

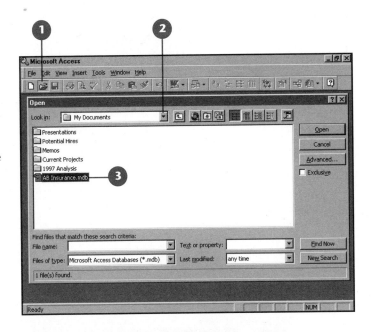

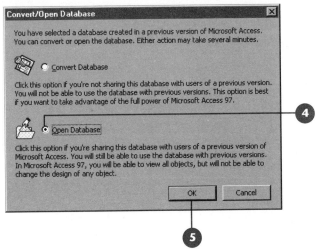

Analyzing a Database

From time to time, you should analyze your database to ensure that it is set up and works as efficiently as possible. Begin by running the *Performance Analyzer*, which provides ways to organize your database optimally and helps you make any necessary adjustments. Whenever you determine that several fields in a table store duplicate information, run the *Table Analyzer* to help you split the data into related tables (called *normalization*), but leave the original table intact.

"How can I make sure my database is performing at its best?"

Optimize Database Performance

1. Open the database you want to analyze.

2. Click the Tools menu, point to Analyze, and then click Performance.

3. Click the All tab.

4. Click to select any number of objects whose performance you want to analyze.

5. Click OK. If the Performance Analyzer has suggestions for improving the selected object(s), it displays them in its analysis results.

6. Click each item and then review its analysis notes.

7. Press and hold Ctrl and click the recommended or suggested optimizations you want to perform.

8. Click Optimize.

9. Click Close.

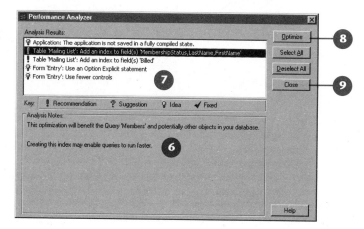

Performance Analyzer results. *The Performance Analyzer returns recommendations, suggestions, and ideas. You should have Access perform the recommended optimizations. Suggested optimizations have potential tradeoffs, and you should review the possible outcomes in the Analysis Notes box before having Access perform them. You must perform idea optimizations manually; just follow the instructions in the Analysis Notes box.*

Analyze the Design of Your Tables

1 Click the Tools menu, point to Analyze, and then click Table.

2 If an explanation screen for the Table Analyzer Wizard opens, read it, click Next, read the second explanation screen, and then click Next.

3 Click the table you want to analyze, and then click Next.

4 Click the option button for letting the wizard decide which fields to place in which tables, and then click Next.

5 Continue following the wizard instructions for naming the new tables, specifying the primary key for the new tables, and so on, and then click Finish; or click Cancel if the wizard recommends not to split the table.

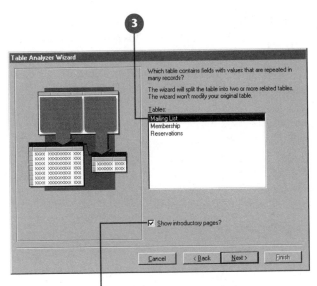

Clear this check box if you don't want to see the two explanation screens of the Table Analyzer Wizard.

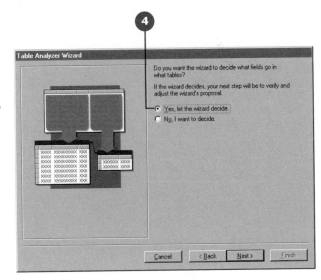

14

Documenting Objects

Sometimes, you'll want to review the design definitions of various database objects. The *Documenter* can compile some or all definitions for you, which you can then save or print.

Document the Design of Database Objects

1 Click the Tools menu, point to Analyze, and then click Documenter.

2 Click the All Object Types tab.

3 Click the check boxes for any number of database objects to select them.

4 Click Options.

5 Click the definitions you want to print for the selected object(s).

6 Click OK.

7 Click OK.

8 Check how many pages will print, and then click the Print button on the Print Preview toolbar.

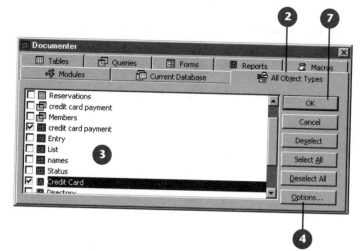

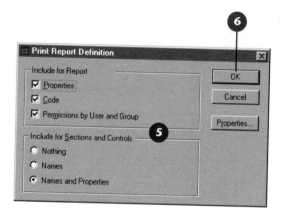

Customizing Access

Although Microsoft Access 97 is designed to be flexible and easy to use, you can customize the program to reflect your own preferences and the way you work. You can customize Access by automating frequent tasks and keystrokes with macros attached to buttons. You can modify the way Access starts to increase your productivity. You can change the toolbars and menus to display the features you use most frequently. You can even create your own dialog boxes to appear when you first start Access. The purpose of each of these customization features is the same—to make Access even easier to use and permit you to accomplish more with less effort.

Creating a Shortcut on the Desktop

You can create a shortcut on your desktop to start Access and open a particular database object. For example, if you are working on a project and you always need to start working in a specific table or run a particular macro right away, you can create a shortcut that performs this operation directly from the desktop.

TRY THIS

Create a shortcut. *Create a shortcut that opens the Employees table in the Northwind database.*

TIP

Rename a shortcut. *You can change the name of a shortcut by clicking the name below the shortcut and then clicking the name again to display the insertion point. Then type the new name.*

Create a Shortcut on the Desktop

1. Select the object that you want to open from the desktop. For example, to open a table from the desktop, display the Database window and select the table.

2. Click the Edit menu, and then click Create Shortcut. The Create Shortcut dialog box specifies the location of the object by default.

3. Click Browse if you want to change the location of the object.

4. Click OK.

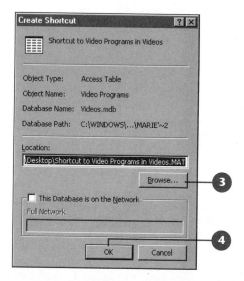

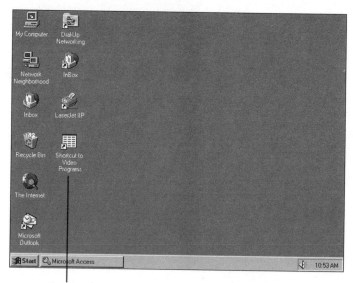

Access places a shortcut icon on the desktop.

Customizing the Menu Bar

You can customize the existing menu bar by adding buttons, commands, and macros that you use frequently. Adding items to the menu bar is a great way to have easy access to the features you need without adding more buttons to an existing toolbar or taking up more space in the program window with additional toolbars. The ability to drag features from different parts of the program window makes it easy to add items to the menu bar.

TIP

The Undo button does not undo when you are customizing a menu bar. *Remember not to click the Undo button while you are customizing a menu bar. Rather than reversing the last change, clicking the Undo button will only select the button so you can copy or move it.*

Customize a Menu Bar

1 Click the View menu, click Toolbars, and then click Customize.

2 From any displayed toolbar or menu bar in the program window, hold down the Ctrl key as you drag each item that you want to add to the menu bar.

If you do not hold down the Ctrl key as you drag, you will remove the command or button from its original location.

3 Click the Commands tab, select a category, click the command that you want to place on the menu bar, and then drag the command to the menu bar.

4 If necessary, remove commands you don't use very often by dragging them from the menu bar back into the Customize dialog box.

5 If you want, rearrange menu items simply by dragging them to a new location on the menu bar.

6 Click the Modify Selection button to change the appearance of an item on the menu bar.

7 Click Close.

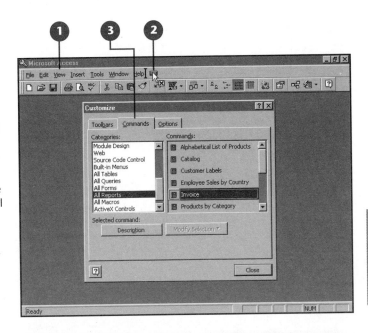

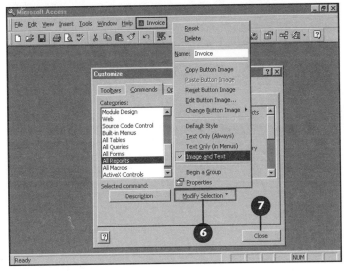

15

Customizing Toolbars

You can customize existing toolbars by adding buttons, commands, and macros that you use frequently. You can also create your own toolbars that contain the features, including macros, that you use often when you are performing a particular task in Access, such as editing records in a table.

TIP

Restore the original commands or buttons to a toolbar or menu bar. *On the Toolbars tab of the Customize dialog box, select (but do not click the check box for) the toolbar or menu you want to restore. Click the Reset button.*

TRY THIS

Hide and display the toolbars you want. *On the Toolbars tab of the Customize dialog box, click the check box for each toolbar you want to display. Clear the check box for each toolbar you want to hide.*

Customize a Toolbar

1. Click the View menu, click Toolbars, and then click Customize.

2. Click the Toolbars tab, and then click the name of the toolbar you want to customize. The toolbar appears below the existing toolbar in the program window.

3. From any displayed toolbar or menu, hold down the Shift key as you drag each toolbar button or menu that you want to add to the customized toolbar.

4. Click the Commands tab, select a category, click the command that you want to place on the toolbar, and then drag the command to the toolbar.

5. If your window is not wide enough to fit new buttons on the toolbar, you can:

   ◆ Adjust the resolution of your monitor.

   ◆ Remove buttons you don't use very often by dragging them from the toolbar back into the Customize dialog box or to another toolbar.

6. Click Close.

Press and hold the Ctrl key if you want to copy the button.

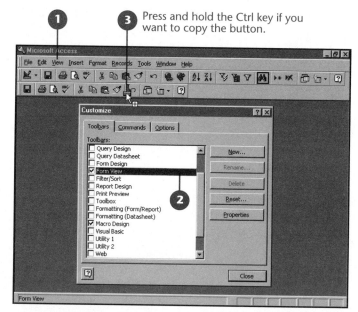

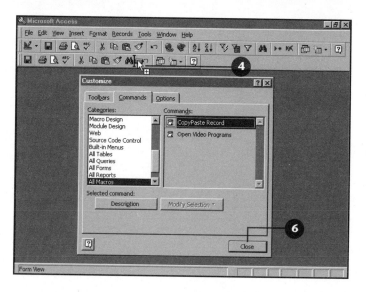

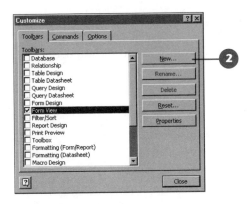

TIP

The Undo button does not undo when you are customizing a toolbar.

Remember not to click the Undo button while you are customizing a toolbar. Rather than reversing the last change, clicking the Undo button will only select the button so you can copy or move it.

TIP

Place a macro on a toolbar.

If you want to place a macro on the toolbar, choose the All Macros category on the Commands tab, and then drag the macro you want to the toolbar.

Create a New Toolbar

1 Click the View menu, click Toolbars, and then click Customize.

2 On the Toolbars tab, click New.

3 Type a name for the new toolbar.

4 Click OK. A new empty toolbar appears in the program window.

5 From any displayed toolbar or menu in the program window, hold down the Ctrl key as you drag each button or menu that you want to add to the new toolbar.

If you do not hold down the Ctrl key as you drag, you will remove the command or button from its original location.

6 Click the Commands tab, select a category, click the command that you want to place on the toolbar, and then drag the command to the toolbar.

7 Click Close.

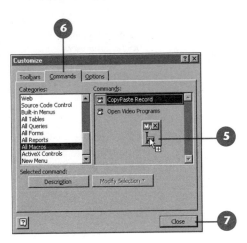

15

Customizing a Database Startup

Another way to customize an Access database is to specify what happens when you first open the database. For example, you can set startup options to choose which menus and commands are available and what title and icon appear in the program title bar. You can also use a *switchboard* instead of, or in addition to, the Database window as another way to navigate between the forms, reports, and other objects in your database. If you use the Database Wizard to create your database, it prepares a Main Switchboard form for you, which you can also display when you start the database.

Set Startup Options

1. Click the Tools menu, and then click Startup.

2. Type the name you want in the title bar.

3. Enter a bitmap (.bmp) or icon (.ico) filename.

4. Select a default menu bar for the open database.

5. Check to display all the built-in menus or clear to hide commands that change the database.

6. Select a custom shortcut menu bar for the open database.

7. Select to display the default toolbars.

8. Clear to disable shortcut menus, the Close button on toolbars, and the Toolbars command on the View menu.

9. Click OK.

10. Open and close the database or restart Access to see the new startup.

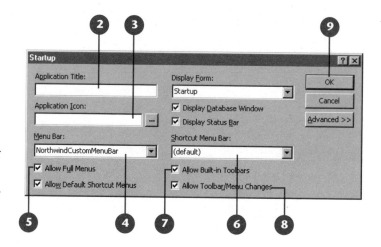

TIP

**View the Main Switch-
board form at any time.**
*Clicking the Forms tab in the
Database window, and then
double-click Main Switchboard.*

SEE ALSO

*See "Adding Functionality with
Add-ins" on page 209 and
"Using Add-Ins" on page 210
for information about creating a
custom switchboard form.*

Show the Main Switchboard

1 Click the Tools menu, and then click Startup.

2 Click the Display Form drop-down arrow.

3 Click Main Switchboard (or another form you want to display), if necessary.

4 To hide the Database window, clear the Display Database Window check box.

5 Click OK.

6 Close, and then open the database to launch the switchboard.

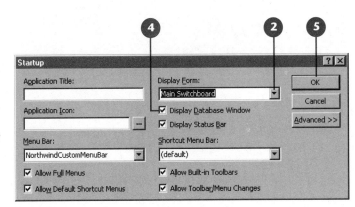

15

Specifying Keyboard and Viewing Options

With the Options command on the Tools menu, you can change a variety of options for many Access features. For example, you can customize the ways in which Access carries out specific editing tasks, and you can determine which features are in effect when you are viewing information in the program window. The Keyboard tab and the View tab of the Options dialog box provides the options that you can set to improve your productivity or suit your preferences as you work in Access.

Viewing options

Keyboard options

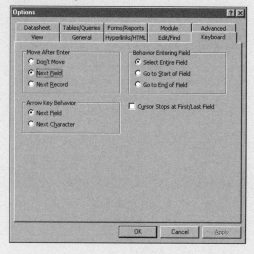

Learning About Macros

A *macro* is a stored collection of actions that perform a particular task, such as opening a specific form and report at the same time, or printing a group of reports. You can create macros to automate a repetitive or complex task, or to automate a series of tasks. By automating repetitive tasks, a macro guarantees consistency and minimizes errors caused when you forget a step. When automating difficult tasks, the macro protects you from unnecessary complexity. By automating a series a tasks in a macro, you have the convenience of performing multiple tasks with a single button or keystroke. For whatever reason you create them, macros can dramatically increase your productivity when working with your database.

Macros consist of actions or commands that are needed to complete the operation you want to automate. Sorting, querying, and printing are examples of *actions*. *Arguments* are additional pieces of information required to carry out an individual action. For example, anOpenTable macro action would require arguments that identify the name of the table you want to open, the view in which to display the table, and the kinds of changes a user would be able to make in this table. Because there are no wizards to help you make a macro, you create a macro by entering actions and arguments directly in Design view. After creating a macro, save your work and name the macro.

A macro in a database

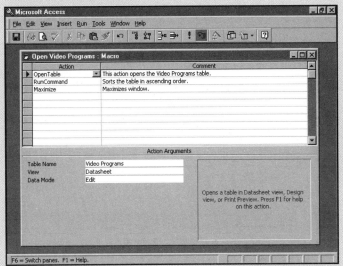

15

Creating a Macro

Before you begin creating a macro, it is a good idea to plan the actions required to successfully complete the tasks you want to automate. Think about the tasks you do most often or the operations that require you to perform a series of tasks. These activities are good candidates for a macro. Then practice the steps needed to carry out the operation and write them down as you go. Finally, test your written instructions by performing each of the steps yourself.

TIP

Run the macro in the correct view. *Keep in mind that a macro will only perform the actions that are appropriate in the currently active view, so be sure to display the correct view before you run the macro. You can also consider having the first action in the macro display the view in which you want to run the macro.*

Create a Macro

1. In the Database window, click the Macros tab, and then click New.

2. Click the Action drop-down arrow, click the action you want to use, and then press Tab. There are several dozen actions from which you can choose.

   One particularly powerful action is the RunCommand action. This action allows you to select from hundreds of Access commands for arguments.

3. If you want to provide a brief explanation of the action, you can type a comment in the Comment column.

4. In the Action Arguments section, click the table name of the first argument box, and then click a value from the drop-down list.

5. Depending on the action you chose in step 2, there might be additional arguments you must provide in this part of the window.

6. To add more actions to the macro, click the right side of a new Action row, and repeat steps 2 through 5. The macro will carry out the actions in the order in which you list them.

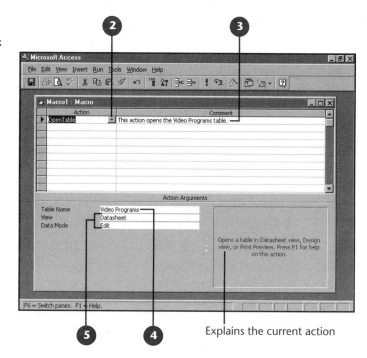

Explains the current action

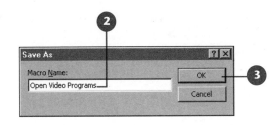

TRY THIS

Review existing macros. *To examine the actions, arguments, and conditions of several existing macros, open the Northwind database, click the Macros tab, click a macro name in the list, and then click Design.*

TIP

Make changes to an existing macro. *Open the macro in Macro Design view, change the necessary actions and arguments, and then save the changes. To insert a new action, click the Insert Rows button on the Macro Design toolbar; remove an action by selecting the action row and then clicking the Delete Rows button. To create a new macro based on an existing one, open the macro in Macro Design view, and then click the Save As command on the File menu. Give the macro a new name and modify the new macro as needed.*

Name and Save a Macro

1. On the Macro Design toolbar, click the Save button.

2. Enter a descriptive macro name that helps identify the tasks the macro carries out.

3. Click OK.

15

Running and Testing a Macro

To have the macro perform its actions, you must run the macro. There are two ways to run a macro. You can have the macro perform all the steps in a sequence at once, or you can test a macro by running it to perform one step at a time, allowing you to review the results of each step. To run all the steps in a sequence, choose the Run Macro command on the Tools menu, or click the Run button on the toolbar. To step through the macro one action at a time, click the Single Step button. After testing your macro, you might discover that it did not perform all its tasks in the way you expected. If so, you can make changes and retest the macro as you continue to make adjustments in Macro Design view.

Run button

Run a Macro in a Sequence

1. Display the macro you want to run in Macro Design view.

    If your macro does not automatically switch you to the correct view, switch to the view in which you want to run the macro.

2. Click the Run button on the toolbar.

    ◆ If you do not see the Run button on the toolbar, click the Tools menu, and then click Run Macro.

    ◆ Click the Macro drop-down arrow, and then double-click the macro you want to run.

3. If the macro encounters an action it cannot perform, you see a message box stating the action it could not carry out. Click OK.

4. In the Action Failed dialog box, click Halt.

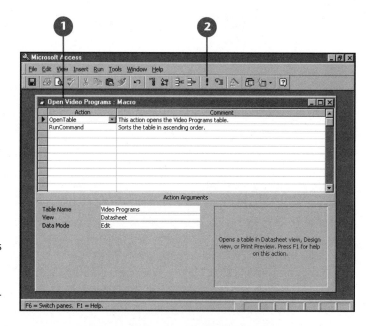

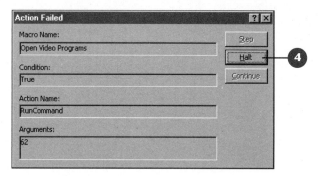

TIP

Run all steps in a macro. *If Single Step is active, you can still run all the steps in the macro without stepping. In the Macro Single Step dialog box, click Continue.*

TIP

Stop the macro before it finishes. *In the Macro Single Step dialog box, click Halt.*

TIP

Run a macro from the Database window. *In the Database window, click the Macros tab, and then double-click the name of the macro you want to run.*

Run button

Testing a Macro Step-by-Step

1 Display the macro you want to run in Macro Design view.

2 Click the Single Step button on the Macro Design toolbar.

If your macro does not automatically switch to the correct view, switch to the view in which you want to run the macro.

3 Click the Run button on the toolbar.

♦ If you do not see the Run button on the toolbar, click the Tools menu, and then click Run Macro.

♦ Click the Macro drop-down arrow, and then double-click the macro you want to run.

4 In Macro Single Step dialog box, click Step to perform the first action in the macro.

5 After the macro performs the step, repeat step 4 until the macro finishes.

6 If the macro encounters an action it cannot perform, you see a message box stating the action it could not carry out. Click OK to close the message box. Click Halt to stop the macro.

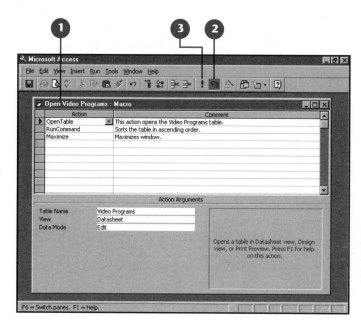

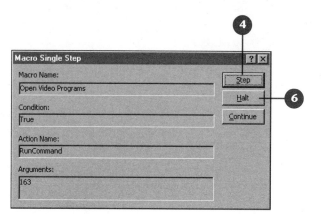

Adding a Macro to a Toolbar

If you use macros and you like using toolbar buttons to complete tasks, you can assign some of your favorite macros to toolbar buttons. Like menu commands, a toolbar button makes a macro just a button click away. Excel offers a choice of custom buttons you can assign to your macros to make it easier to remember what each represents.

SEE ALSO

See "Learning About Macros" on page 225 and "Creating a Macro" on page 226 for more information on macros and how to record them.

Assign a Button to a Macro

1 Click the View menu, point to Toolbars, and then click Customize.

2 Make sure the toolbar you want to add a button to is displayed.

3 Click the Commands tab.

4 Click Macros from the Categories list.

5 Click Custom Button from the Commands list.

6 Drag the button to a toolbar.

7 Click Modify Selection.

8 Click Assign Macro.

9 Click the macro you want to use in the Assign Macro dialog box.

10 Click OK.

11 Click Close.

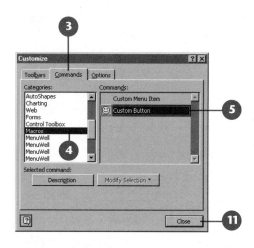

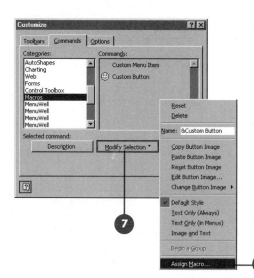

SEE ALSO

See "Customizing Toolbars" on page 220 for information on creating a new toolbar.

Change a Button's Appearance

1. Click the View menu, point to Toolbars, and then click Customize.

2. Make sure the toolbar you want is displayed.

3. Click the button on the toolbar you want to change.

4. Click the Commands tab.

5. Click Modify Selection.

6. Point to Change Button Image.

7. Click a new button on the palette.

8. Click Close.

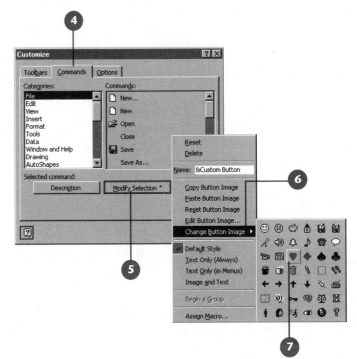

15

Index

AutoForm command (Database toolbar), creating forms, 130, 133
AutoForm Wizards, creating forms, 130, 132-33
AutoFormat button (Design view), 111, 139
formatting forms/reports, 151
AutoNumber data type, 83
AutoNumber fields, appending records to tables with, 63
AutoReport command (Database toolbar), creating reports, 113
AutoReport Wizards, creating reports, 110, 112

background colors, of forms/ reports, 155
beeps, on entering records, 91
Blank Database option, creating database files, 73
bold typeface, applying, 150
borders
changing thickness, 153
coloring/coloring inside, 154
creating, 141, 149, 152
making transparent, 154
resizing, 152
bound controls
in forms, 131
in reports, 116, 117
Bound Object Frame button (Design View Toolbox), 141
buttons
creating command buttons, 141
navigation buttons (Table windows), 30

view buttons (Access window), 138
See also option buttons; toolbar buttons

calculated controls
in forms, 131
in reports, 116
calculated fields, renaming, 60
calculations
in queries, 60
in reports, 120-21
capitalization
correcting with AutoCorrect, 96
matching in searches, 34
Caption property, setting, 88
Cascade Delete Related Records option (Relationships dialog box), 197
Cascade Update Related Fields option (Relationships dialog box), 197
cascading Table windows, 22
cell contents (in Graph), editing, 176
cells (in Graph), 172
characters
deleting, 98
specifying column widths in, 29
Chart Type dialog box (Graph), 174, 175
Chart Wizard, creating Graph charts, 172-73
Check Box button (Design View Toolbox), 140
check boxes
creating, 140
selecting, 12

clip art
getting from the Web, 189
inserting, 149, 166
Clip Gallery, downloading media clips to, 189
clip media
getting from the Web, 189
See also clip art; pictures
Clipboard
copying and pasting records, 94, 95
copying/cutting and pasting objects via, 158, 159
moving text, 99
Close button (Table windows), 21
closing
databases, 18, 75, 203
tables, 21
coloring
forms/reports, 149, 154-55
lines/borders, 154
text, 155
colors
background colors, 155
hyperlink colors, 193
column headings
aligning with report controls, 119
changing without changing field names, 61
Column Width dialog box, 28
column widths
resizing, 28, 119
specifying, 29
columns (in reports), changing spacing between, 118
columns (in tables)
freezing/unfreezing, 26
hiding/redisplaying, 27
moving, 25
resizing, 28
See also fields (in tables)

Combo Box button (Design View Toolbox), 141
combo boxes, creating, 141, 144-45
Command Button button (Design View Toolbox), 141
command buttons, creating, 141
common fields (in multiple tables), 72, 196, 197
Compact Database Into dialog box, 204
compacting databases, 204
comparison expressions, in queries, 58
Contents tab (Help Topics dialog box), 14
control wizards
creating controls, 131, 144-45
displaying, 140
Control Wizards button (Design View Toolbox), 140
controls
applying special effects to, 148, 149, 156
formatting, 119, 131
and labels, 131
moving, 118-19, 121, 142
resizing, 118-19, 142
selecting, 143
See also ActiveX controls; form controls; report controls
Convert Database Into dialog box, 212
Convert/Open Database dialog box, 213
converting previous-version databases, 212, 213
versus enabling, 213
copying, objects, 159

wizards, *continued*
  Crosstab Query Wizard,
      54-55
  Database Wizards, 73, 74-75
  Form Wizard, 130, 134-35
  Import Spreadsheet
      Wizard, 102
  Link Spreadsheet
      Wizard, 103
  List Box Wizard, 144-45
  Publish to the Web
      Wizard, 192
  Query Wizard, 46, 48-49
  Report Wizard, 110, 114-15,
      122-23
  Simple Query Wizard, 48-49
  Table Analyzer Wizard,
      214, 215
  Table Wizard, 76, 78-79,
      80, 81
Word (Microsoft), viewing Word
      files, 187
Word documents
  creating from databases, 107
  inserting Access data
      into, 106
World Wide Web. *See* Web

Yes/No data type, 83, 140

Marie Swanson has authored more than 25 books, including Microsoft Word 6.0, Word 95, and Word 97 Step-by-Step books (Microsoft Press). She has also written the Step-by-Step books for Microsoft Project for Windows, versions 3.0, 4.0, and 4.1, and Microsoft FoxPro 2.5 for Windows. With fifteen years experience in corporate PC support and training environments, Marie and her company, WriteWorks, have written customized training materials and end-user documentation for internal accounting systems, image retrieval applications, as well as for major software packages.

Acknowledgments

In addition to my assistants who provided valuable support on other projects while I completed this At a Glance effort, I would like to extend my deepest thanks to Kathy Finnegan, the development editor and Jane Pedicini, the copyeditor. Without the guidance and review of these individuals, this work would have been impossible. Also, "thank you" to Robin Geller who came to the rescue (when I had run out words and energy) and lent her expertise to write the last two sections of this book. Of course, the greatest thanks must go to the people at Perspection, Inc., who provided me the opportunity to work on this project and who shepherded the entire process.

The manuscript for this book was prepared and submitted to Microsoft Press in electronic form. Text files were prepared using Microsoft Word for Windows 95. Pages were composed by Steven Payne, Patricia Young, and Gary Bedard using PageMaker for Windows, with text in Stone Sans and display type in Stone Serif and Stone Serif Semibold. Composed pages were delivered to the printer as electronic prepress files.

Cover Designer
Tim Girvin Design

Interior Graphic Designer
designlab
Kim Eggleston

Graphic Layout
Steven Payne

Principal Compositor
Patricia Young

Compositor
Gary Bedard

Indexer
Michael Brackney